The Language
of SQL

Second Edition

Larry Rockoff

✦✦Addison-Wesley

Hoboken, NJ • Boston • Indianapolis • San Francisco
New York • Toronto • Montreal • London • Munich • Paris • Madrid
Cape Town • Sydney • Tokyo • Singapore • Mexico City

The Language of SQL, Second Edition

Copyright © 2017 by Pearson Education, Inc.

ISBN-13: 978-0-13-465825-4

ISBN-10: 0-13-465825-6

Library of Congress Control Number: 2016945436

Printed in the United States of America

3   17

Trademarks

All terms mentioned in this book that are known to be trademarks or service marks have been appropriately capitalized. The publisher cannot attest to the accuracy of this information. Use of a term in this book should not be regarded as affecting the validity of any trademark or service mark.

Warning and Disclaimer

Every effort has been made to make this book as complete and as accurate as possible, but no warranty or fitness is implied. The information provided is on an "as is" basis. The author and the publisher shall have neither liability nor responsibility to any person or entity with respect to any loss or damages arising from the information contained in this book.

Special Sales

For information about buying this title in bulk quantities, or for special sales opportunities (which may include electronic versions; custom cover designs; and content particular to your business, training goals, marketing focus, or branding interests), please contact our corporate sales department at corpsales@pearsoned.com or (800) 382-3419.

For government sales inquiries, please contact governmentsales@pearsoned.com.

For questions about sales outside the U.S., please contact intlcs@pearson.com.

Editor
Mark Taber

Project and Copy Editor
Dan Foster,
Scribe Tribe

Technical Editor
Siddhartha Singh

Designer
Chuti Prasertsith

Compositor
Danielle Foster,
Scribe Tribe

Indexer
Valerie Haynes
Perry

Proofreader
Scout Festa

Contents at a Glance

Table of Contents

About the Author

Larry Rockoff has been involved with SQL and business intelligence development for many years. His main area of interest is in using reporting tools to explore and analyze data in complex databases. He holds an MBA from the University of Chicago, with a specialization in management science. He currently works with data warehouse and reporting applications for a major retail pharmacy.

Besides writing about SQL, he has also published books on Microsoft Access and Excel.

He also maintains a website that features book reviews on technology topics, focusing on analytics and business intelligence as well as broader societal issues, at

larryrockoff.com

Please feel free to visit that site to contact the author with any comments or questions. You are also encouraged to follow his Facebook author page or Twitter site at

facebook.com/larryrockoff
twitter.com/larryrockoff

Acknowledgments

A huge thanks goes out to all at Pearson who assisted with this book. I'd like to specifically thank Mark Taber, who was instrumental in bringing this book to Pearson from my previous publisher. I'd also like to thank project editor and copy editor Dan Foster, as well as Danielle Foster, who was responsible for the page layout. Siddhartha Singh did a superb job on the technical review. Chuti Prasertsith provided a wonderfully vibrant cover design. Finally, I must mention the generally thankless but essential tasks of the book's indexer, Valerie Haynes Perry, and proofreader, Scout Festa.

As this is a second edition, I'd also like to thank all readers of the first edition, and especially those individuals who have contacted me at larryrockoff.com and offered gracious comments as to the usefulness of the book in their personal lives. It's both humbling and thrilling to realize that your thoughts on a relatively mundane topic can assist someone halfway around the world.

We Want to Hear from You!

As the reader of this book, *you* are our most important critic and commentator. We value your opinion and want to know what we're doing right, what we could do better, what areas you'd like to see us publish in, and any other words of wisdom you're willing to pass our way.

We welcome your comments. You can email or write directly to let us know what you did or didn't like about this book—as well as what we can do to make our books better.

Please note that we cannot help you with technical problems related to the topic of this book, and that due to the high volume of mail we receive, we might not be able to reply to every message.

When you write, please be sure to include this book's title and author, as well as your name and phone number or email address.

Email: feedback@developers-library.info

Mail: Reader Feedback
        Addison-Wesley Developer's Library
        800 East 96th Street
        Indianapolis, IN 46240 USA

Reader Services

Visit our website and register this book at www.informit.com/register for convenient access to any updates, downloads, or errata that might be available for this book.

Introduction

SQL, or Structured Query Language, is the primary language used to communicate with relational databases. The goal of this book is to serve as a useful introductory guide to this essential language.

In an alternate universe, the title of this book might have been *The Logic of SQL*. This is because, like all computer languages, the language of SQL has much more to do with cold hard logic than with English vocabulary. Nevertheless, the word *language* has been retained in the title for a number of reasons. First, a certain language-based syntax in SQL distinguishes it from other computer languages. Unlike other languages, SQL employs many ordinary words, such as WHERE and FROM, as keywords in its syntax.

In the spirit of the language embedded in SQL, we've adopted an emphasis on language in our sequence of topics. With this book, you'll learn SQL as you would learn English. SQL keywords are presented in a logical progression, from simple to more complex. In essence, this is an attempt to deal with language and logic simultaneously.

To learn any language, one must begin by hearing and remembering the actual words that form the basis of its utterance. At the same time, those words have a certain meaning that must be understood. In the case of SQL, the meaning has a great deal to do with logic.

One final reason for persisting with the title *The Language of SQL* rather than *The Logic of SQL* is that it simply sounds better. While there can be few literary pretensions in a computer-language book, the hope is that the presence of the word language will generate some additional enthusiasm for a subject that is, after all, quite interesting.

Topics and Features

Even if you're not yet familiar with SQL, suffice it to say that it is a complex language with many components and features. In this book, we'll focus on one main topic:

- How to use SQL to retrieve data from a database

To a lesser extent, we will also cover:

- How to update data in a database
- How to build and maintain databases
- How to design relational databases
- Strategies for displaying data after it has been retrieved

A number of features make this book unique among introductory SQL books:

- **You will not be required to download software or sit with a computer as you read the text.**

  Our intent is to provide examples of SQL usage that can be understood simply by reading the book. The text includes small data samples that allow you to clearly see how SQL statements work.

- **A language-based approach is employed to enable you to learn SQL as you would learn English.**

  Topics are organized in an intuitive and logical sequence. SQL keywords are introduced one at a time, allowing you to build on your prior understanding as you encounter new words and concepts.

- **This book covers the syntax of three widely used databases: Microsoft SQL Server, MySQL, and Oracle.**

  If there are any differences between these databases, the Microsoft SQL Server syntax is shown in the main text. Special "Database Differences" sidebars show and explain any variations in the syntax for MySQL or Oracle.

- **An emphasis is given to relevant aspects of SQL for retrieving data.**

  This approach is useful for those who need only to use SQL in conjunction with a reporting tool. In our final chapter, we'll move beyond pure SQL to cover strategies for displaying data after it has been retrieved, including ideas on how to use crosstab reports and pivot tables. In the real world, these types of tools can substantially lessen the burden on the SQL developer and provide greater flexibility for the end user.

> **Note**
>
> Visit our website and register this book at informit.com/register for convenient access to downloads, updates, or errata that may be available for this book.

What's New in the Second Edition

Here are some of the new features of this second edition:

- **Coverage of the latest database versions**

  All syntax and examples have been taken from the latest versions of the three main databases covered in this book: Microsoft SQL Server 2016, MySQL 5.7, and Oracle 12c.

- **Coverage of subtotals and crosstabs**

  We added a new chapter on subtotals and crosstabs to provide additional possibilities for summarizing data. This material allows users to add subtotals and running totals to their queries. Additionally, exposure to SQL crosstab queries allows for a greater appreciation of the value of pivot tables, which are covered toward the end of the book.

- **Coverage of ranking functions**

  We added new material on ranking functions. This important class of functions permits users to produce row numbers and calculate percentiles. A related capability is the ability to divide data into partitions prior to the application of ranking functions.

- **Expanded coverage of conditional logic**

  Our first edition included some basic material on the CASE expression and conditional logic. This topic is often excluded from introductory SQL books but nevertheless has tremendous practical value for any SQL developer. This second edition adds a number of new examples in Chapters 8 and 9 of how the CASE expression can be employed.

- **New and more consistent datasets**

  As in the first edition, each chapter has its own small set of data for examples. However, unlike before, this second edition now uses a consistent set of datasets for all chapters. A Customers table referenced in one chapter will be the same as a Customers table in any other chapter. If you wish to load sample data for testing, you can now run a single script to load all data at once. The previous edition required separate scripts for each chapter.

- **Other improvements**

  A few other noteworthy topics have been added, including common table expressions and comments. Terminology throughout the book has been modified for greater consistency and conformity with standard usage. Finally, an overview of the SELECT statement has been added early in Chapter 2, to give you a better idea of the topics to come.

Plan of the Book

This book presents its topics in a unique sequence. The majority of SQL books run through their topics as if you were a database administrator who needs to create and design a database from scratch, then load the database with data, and then finally start to retrieve that data. In this book, we start right off with data retrieval, and then come around to database design in the final chapters. This is done as a motivational tactic, allowing you to quickly get into interesting topics related to data retrieval before having to deal with the more arcane subjects of indexes and foreign keys.

The 20 chapters in the book can be broken down into a number of broad sections:

- Chapter 1 presents introductory material about relational databases that is necessary to understand before encountering the SELECT statement.
- Chapters 2 through 5 begin an exploration of the SELECT statement, covering the basics of calculations, functions, and sorting.

- Chapters 6 through 8 deal with selection criteria, from simple Boolean logic to conditional logic.
- Chapters 9 and 10 explore ways to summarize data, from simple counts to more complex aggregations and subtotals.
- Chapters 11 through 15 discuss ways to retrieve data from multiple tables via joins, subqueries, views, and set logic.
- Chapters 16 through 18 move beyond the SELECT statement to focus on broader topics associated with relational databases, such as stored procedures, updates, and table maintenance.
- Finally, Chapters 19 and 20 bring us back to the basics of database design and then to strategies for displaying data.

Appendixes A, B, and C provide information on how to get started with each of the three databases covered in the book: Microsoft SQL Server, Oracle, and MySQL.

Companion Website

A listing of all SQL statements in this book can be found at this site:

- **www.informit.com/store/language-of-sql-9780134658254**

These three files are provided:

- SQL Statements for Microsoft SQL Server
- SQL Statements for MySQL
- SQL Statements for Oracle

These three files list all SQL statements in the book for each of these databases. Additionally, these files contain a SQL script that allows you to create all the data used in the book. After running the setup script, you can execute statements in the book and see the same output.

Instructions on how to execute the setup script are provided within each of the files.

1

Relational Databases and SQL

As mentioned in the Introduction, SQL is the most widely used software tool for communicating with data residing in relational databases. In this endeavor, SQL utilizes elements of both language and logic. As a language, SQL employs a unique syntax with many English words, such as WHERE, FROM, and HAVING. As an expression of logic, it specifies the details of how data in a relational database is to be retrieved or updated.

With this duality in mind, we attempt in this book to emphasize both language and logic components as we present the topics that make up SQL. In all languages, whether they be computer or spoken, there are actual words to be learned and remembered. As such, we will present the various keywords present in SQL one at a time in a logical sequence. As we progress through each chapter, you'll build on your prior vocabulary to learn new keywords and exciting possibilities for interactions with a database.

In addition to the words themselves, there is also logic to be considered. The words employed by SQL have a distinct logical meaning and intent. The logic of SQL is just as important as the language. As in all computer languages, there is frequently more than one way to specify any desired objective. The nuances of what is possible encompass both the language and logic involved.

Let's start with the language. Once you become familiar with the syntax of SQL, you might find yourself thinking of SQL commands as analogous to English sentences and having a certain expressive meaning.

For example, compare this sentence:

```
I would like a hamburger and fries
from your value menu,
and make it to go.
```

with this SQL statement:

```
Select city, state
from Customers
order by state
```

We'll get into the details later, but this SQL statement means that we want the city and state fields from a table named Customers in a database, and we want the results sorted by state.

In both cases, we're specifying which items we want (hamburger/fries or city/state), where we want it from (value menu or Customers table), and some extra instructions (make it to go, or sort the results by state).

But before we get started, let's address one minor point: how to pronounce the word SQL. It turns out that there are two choices. One option is to simply to say it as individual letters, like "S-Q-L." Another possibility, preferred by the author, is to pronounce it as the word "sequel." This is one less syllable, and a little easier to say. However, there's no real agreement on the question. It's basically a matter of personal preference.

As for what the letters S-Q-L mean, most agree that they stand for "Structured Query Language." However, even here, there is not total agreement. Some would argue that SQL stands for nothing at all, since the language is derived from an old language from IBM called sequel, which did not, in fact, stand for structured query language.

What Is SQL?

So what is SQL? In a nutshell, SQL is a standard computer language for maintaining and utilizing data in relational databases. Put simply, SQL is a language that lets users interact with relational databases. It has a long history of development by various organizations going back to the 1970s. In 1986, the American National Standards Institute (ANSI) published its first set of standards regarding the language, and it has gone through several revisions since that time.

Generally speaking, there are three major components of the SQL language. The first is called *DML*, or *Data Manipulation Language*. This module of the language allows you to retrieve, update, add, or delete data in a database. The second component is called *DDL*, or *Data Definition Language*. DDL enables you to create and modify the database itself. For example, DDL provides ALTER statements that let you modify the design of tables in a database. Finally, the third component, *DCL*, or *Data Control Language*, maintains proper security for the database.

Major software vendors, such as Microsoft and Oracle, have adapted the standard for their own purposes and have added numerous extensions and modifications to the language. But although each vendor has its own unique interpretation of SQL, there is still an underlying base language, which is much the same for all vendors. That base language is what we'll cover in this book.

As a computer language, SQL is different from other languages you may be familiar with, such as Visual Basic or C++. These languages tend to be *procedural* in nature, meaning that they allow you to specify specific procedures to accomplish a desired task. SQL is more of a *declarative* language. In SQL, the desired objective is often declared with a single statement. The simpler structure of SQL is possible because it is concerned only with relational databases rather than the entirety of computer systems.

One additional point of clarification about the SQL language is that it is sometimes confused with specific SQL databases. Many software companies sell database management systems (DBMS) software. In common usage, the databases in these types of software packages are often referred to as *SQL databases*, because the SQL language is the primary means of managing and accessing data in these databases. Some vendors even use the word *SQL* as part of the database name. For example, Microsoft calls its latest database *SQL Server 2016*. But in fact, SQL is more properly a language than a database. Our focus in this book is on the language of SQL rather than on any particular database.

Microsoft SQL Server, MySQL, and Oracle

Although our aim is to cover the core language of SQL as it applies to all implementations, we must ultimately also provide specific examples of SQL syntax. And because syntax does vary somewhat among vendors, we've decided to focus on the SQL syntax utilized by these three popular databases:

- Microsoft SQL Server
- MySQL
- Oracle

In most cases, these databases have the same syntax. However, there are occasional differences. If there is any variance between these databases, the syntax for Microsoft SQL Server will be presented in the main text of this book. Any differences for MySQL or Oracle will be indicated in a sidebar titled "Database Differences," as shown here:

Database Differences

A sidebar such as this will appear whenever there are syntax differences for MySQL or Oracle. The syntax for Microsoft SQL Server will appear in the main text.

Microsoft SQL Server is available in several versions and editions. The most recent version is called *Microsoft SQL Server 2016*. Available editions run from a basic Express edition to a fully featured Enterprise edition. The Express edition is free but still has an abundance of features that allow users to get started with full-fledged database development. The Enterprise edition includes many sophisticated database management features, plus powerful business intelligence components.

Although owned by Oracle, MySQL is an open-source database, which means that no single organization controls its development. MySQL is available on numerous platforms other than Windows, such as Mac OS X and Linux. MySQL offers its Community Edition as a free download. The most recent version is MySQL 5.7.

The Oracle database is available in several editions. The most recent version is called *Oracle Database 12c*. The free version of the database is called the Express edition.

When starting out, it is sometimes useful to download the database of your choice, so you have something to experiment with. However, this book does not require you to do that. The material in this book has been written in such a way as to allow you to learn SQL simply by reading through the text. We'll provide enough data in the text so that you can understand the results of various SQL statements without having to download software and type in statements yourself.

Nevertheless, if you would like to download the free versions of any of these databases, we've included three appendixes with useful instructions and tips on how to do that. Appendix A has complete information on how to get started with Microsoft SQL Server. The instructions include details on how to install the software and execute SQL commands. Similarly, Appendixes B and C cover MySQL and Oracle.

As mentioned in the Introduction, our companion website provides supplemental material that lists all the SQL statements shown in this book in all three databases. However, it's likely that you'll find it unnecessary to download or view the additional material on the companion website. The examples shown throughout this book are self-explanatory and don't require you to do anything else in order to understand the material. However, if you are so inclined, feel free to take advantage of these extra features.

It should also be mentioned that, in addition to SQL Server, MySQL, and Oracle, other popular relational databases are worthy of consideration. For example:

- DB2, from IBM
- Informix, from IBM
- SQL Anywhere, from Sybase
- PostgreSQL, an open-source database
- Microsoft Access, from Microsoft

Of these databases, Microsoft Access is somewhat unique in that it has a graphical element. In essence, Access is a graphical interface for relational databases. In other words, Access allows you to create a query against a relational database entirely through graphical means. A useful aspect of Access for beginners is that you can easily create a query in a visual way and then switch to a SQL view to see the SQL statement you just created. Another distinction of Access is that it is primarily a desktop database. As such, you can use it to create a database that resides entirely in a single file on your PC, but it also allows you to connect to databases created with other tools, such as Microsoft SQL Server.

Relational Databases

With these preliminaries out of the way, let's now look at the basics of relational databases to see how they work. A relational database is a collection of data, stored in any number of tables. In common usage, the term *relational* can be taken to indicate that the tables are usually related to each other in some manner. However, in more precise terms, *relational* refers to mathematical relation theory, and has to do with logical properties that govern the manner in which tables are related.

As an example, let's take the simple case of a database consisting of only two tables: Customers and Orders. The Customers table contains one record for each customer who ever placed an order. The Orders table has one record for each order. Each table can contain any number of fields, which are used to store the various attributes associated with each record. For example, a Customers table might contain fields such as FirstName and LastName.

At this point, it's useful to visualize some tables and the data they contain. The common custom is to display a table as a grid of rows and columns. Each row represents a record in the table. Each column represents a field in the table. The top header row normally contains the field names. The remaining rows show the actual data.

In SQL terminology, records and fields are referred to as *rows* and *columns*, corresponding to the visual representation. So henceforth, we'll use the terms *rows* and *columns* rather than *records* and *fields* to describe the design of tables in relational databases.

Let's look at an example of the simplest possible relational database. This database includes only two tables: Customers and Orders. This is what the Customers table might look like:

CustomerID	FirstName	LastName
1	Bob	Davis
2	Natalie	Lopez
3	Connie	King

The Orders table might appear as:

OrderID	CustomerID	OrderAmount
1	1	50.00
2	1	60.00
3	2	33.50
4	3	20.00

In this example, the Customers table contains three columns: CustomerID, FirstName, and LastName. There are currently three rows in the table, representing Bob Davis, Natalie Lopez, and Connie King. Each row represents a different customer, and each column represents a different piece of information about the customer. Similarly, the Orders table has three columns and four rows. This indicates that there are four orders in the database and three attributes for those orders.

Of course, this example is highly simplistic and only hints at the type of data that could be stored in a real database. For example, a Customers table would normally contain many additional columns describing other attributes of a customer, such as city, state, zip, and phone number. Similarly, an Orders table would ordinarily have columns describing additional attributes of the order, such as order date, sales tax, and the salesperson who took the order.

Primary and Foreign Keys

Note the first column in each table: CustomerID in the Customers table, and OrderID in the Orders table. These columns are commonly referred to as *primary keys*. Primary keys are useful and necessary for two reasons. First, they enable us to uniquely identify a single row in a table. For example, if we wanted to retrieve the row for Bob Davis, we could simply use the CustomerID column to obtain the data. Primary keys also ensure uniqueness. Designating the CustomerID column as a primary key guarantees that this column will have a unique value for every row in the table. Even if we happened to have two different men both named Bob Davis in our database, those rows would have different values in the CustomerID column.

In this example, the values in the primary key columns don't have any particular meaning. In the Customers table, the CustomerID column contains the values 1, 2, and 3 for the three rows in the table. Database tables are often designed in such a way as to generate sequential numbers automatically for the primary key column as new rows are added to the table. This design feature is usually referred to as *auto-increment*.

A second reason for primary keys is that they allow us to easily relate one table to another. In this example, the CustomerID column in the Orders table points to a corresponding row in the Customers table. Looking at the fourth row of the Orders table, notice that the CustomerID column has a value of 3. This means that this order is for the customer with a CustomerID of 3, who happens to be Connie King. The use of common columns among tables is an essential design element in relational databases.

In addition to merely pointing to the Customers table, the CustomerID column in the Orders table can be designated as something called a *foreign key*. We'll cover foreign keys in detail in Chapter 18, "Maintaining Tables," but for now, just be aware that foreign keys can be defined in order to ensure that the column has a valid value. As an example, you would not want the CustomerID column in the Orders table to have a particular value unless that CustomerID actually exists in the Customer table. The designation of a column as a foreign key can accomplish that restriction.

Datatypes

Primary and foreign keys add structure to a database table. They ensure that all tables in a database are accessible and properly related to each other. Another important attribute of every column in a table is its datatype.

Datatypes are simply a way of defining the type of data that the column can contain. A datatype must be specified for each column in every table. Unfortunately, there is a great deal of variation between relational databases as to which datatypes are allowed and what they mean. For example, Microsoft SQL Server, MySQL, and Oracle each have over 30 different allowable datatypes.

It would be impossible to cover the details and nuances of every available datatype, even for just these three databases. What we'll do, however, is summarize the situation by discussing the main categories of datatypes common to most databases. Once you understand the important datatypes in these categories, you will have little trouble with other datatypes you may encounter. Generally, there are three important kinds of datatypes: numeric, character, and date/time.

Numeric datatypes come in a variety of flavors, including bits, integers, decimals, and real numbers. Bits are numeric datatypes that allow for only two values: 0 and 1. Bit datatypes are often used to define an attribute as having a simple true or false type of value. Integers are numbers without decimal places. Decimal datatypes can contain decimal places. Unlike bits, integers, and decimals, real numbers are those numbers whose exact value is only approximately defined internally. The one distinguishing characteristic of all numeric datatypes is that they can be included in arithmetic calculations. Here are a few representative examples of numeric datatypes from Microsoft SQL Server, MySQL, and Oracle.

General Description	Microsoft SQL Server Datatype	MySQL Datatype	Oracle Datatype	Example
bit	bit	bit	(none)	1
integer	int	int	number	43
decimal	decimal	decimal	number	58.63
real	float	float	number	80.62345

Character datatypes are sometimes referred to as *string* or *character string* datatypes. Unlike numeric datatypes, character datatypes aren't restricted to numbers. They can include any alphabetic or numeric digit, and can even contain special characters, such as asterisks. When providing a value for character datatypes in SQL statements, the value must always be surrounded by single quotes. In contrast, numeric datatypes never use quotes. Here are a few representative examples of character datatypes:

General Description	Microsoft SQL Server Datatype	MySQL Datatype	Oracle Datatype	Example
variable length	varchar	varchar	varchar2	'Walt Disney'
fixed length	char	char	char	'60601'

The second example (60601) is presumably a zip code. At first glance, this looks like it might be a numeric datatype because it's composed only of numbers. This is not an unusual situation. Even though they contain only numbers, zip codes are usually defined as character datatypes because there is never a need to perform arithmetic calculations with zip codes.

Date/time datatypes are used for the representation of dates and times. Like character datatypes, date/time datatypes must be enclosed in single quotes. These datatypes allow for special calculations involving dates. For example, a special function can be used to calculate the number of days between any two date/time dates. Here are a few examples of date/time datatypes:

General Description	Microsoft SQL Server Datatype	MySQL Datatype	Oracle Datatype	Example
date	date	date	(none)	'2017-02-15'
date and time	datetime	datetime	date	'2017-02-15 08:48:30'

NULL Values

Another important attribute of individual columns in a table is whether that column is allowed to contain null values. A null value means that there is no data for that particular data element. It literally contains no data. However, null values are not the same as spaces or blanks. Logically, null values and empty spaces are treated differently. The nuances of retrieving data that contains null values will be addressed in detail in Chapter 7, "Boolean Logic."

Many databases will display the word NULL in all capital letters when displaying data with null values. This is done so the user can tell that the data contains a null value and not simply spaces. We will follow that convention and display the word NULL throughout this book to emphasize that it represents that unique type of value.

Primary keys in a database can never contain NULL values. That is because primary keys, by definition, must contain unique values.

The Significance of SQL

Before leaving the general subject of relational databases, let's look at a brief historical overview in order to provide an appreciation of the usefulness of relational databases and the significance of SQL.

Back in the early days of computing in the 1960s, data was typically stored either on magnetic tape or in files on disk drives. Computer programs, written in languages such as FORTRAN and COBOL, typically read through input files and processed one record at a time, eventually moving data to output files. Processing was necessarily complex because procedures needed to be broken down into many individual steps involving temporary tables, sorting, and multiple passes through data until the desired output could be produced.

In the 1970s, advances were made as hierarchical and network databases were invented and utilized. These newer databases, through an elaborate system of internal pointers, made it easier to read through data. For example, a program could read a record for a customer, automatically be pointed to all orders for that customer, and then to all details for each order. But basically that data still needed to be processed one record at a time.

The main problem with data storage prior to relational databases was not how the data was stored, but how it was accessed. The real breakthrough with relational databases came when the language of SQL was developed, because it allowed for an entirely new method of accessing data.

Unlike earlier data retrieval methods, SQL permitted the user to access a large set of data at once. With a single statement, a SQL command could retrieve or update thousands of records from multiple tables. This eliminated a great deal of complexity. Computer programs no longer needed to read one record at a time in a special sequence, while deciding what to do with each record. What used to require hundreds of lines of programming code could now be accomplished with just a few lines of logic.

Looking Ahead

This first chapter provided some background information about relational databases, allowing us to move on to the main topic of retrieving data from databases. We discussed a number of important characteristics of relational databases, such as primary keys, foreign keys, and datatypes. We also talked about the possible existence of NULL values in data. We'll add to our discussion of NULL values in Chapter 7, "Boolean Logic," and return to the general topics of database maintenance in Chapter 18, "Maintaining Tables," and database design in Chapter 19, "Principles of Database Design."

Why is the important topic of database design postponed until much later in this book? In short, this approach is taken so you can plunge into using SQL without having to worry about the details of design at the beginning. In truth, database design is as much an art as it is a science. The principles of database design will hopefully be much more meaningful after you've become more aware of the details and nuances of retrieving some data via SQL. Therefore, we'll temporarily ignore the question of how to design a database and commence with data retrieval in our next chapter.

2

Basic Data Retrieval

Keywords Introduced

SELECT · FROM

In this chapter, we'll begin our exploration of the most important topic in SQL—namely, how to retrieve data from a database. Regardless the size of your organization, the most common request made of SQL developers is the request for a report. Of course, it's a nontrivial exercise to get data into a database, but once the data is there, the energies of business analysts turn to the wealth of data at their disposal and the desire to extract useful information from all that data.

The emphasis in this book on data retrieval corresponds to these real-world demands. Your knowledge of SQL will go a long way toward helping your organization unlock the secrets hidden in the data stored in your databases.

A Simple SELECT

The ability to retrieve data in SQL is accomplished through something called the SELECT statement. Without any preliminary explanation, here is an example of the simplest possible SELECT statement:

```
SELECT * FROM Customers
```

In the SQL language, as in all computer languages, certain words are *keywords*. These words have special meanings and must be used in a particular way. In this statement, the words SELECT and FROM are keywords. The SELECT keyword indicates the start of a SELECT statement. The FROM keyword is used to designate the table from which data is to be retrieved. The name of the table follows the FROM. In this case, the table name is Customers. The asterisk (*) in this example is a special symbol that means "all columns."

As is custom, we'll print keywords in all capital letters. This is done to ensure that they are noticeable. To sum up, this statement means: Select all columns from the Customers table.

If the Customers table looks like this:

CustomerID	FirstName	LastName
1	Sara	Davis
2	Rumi	Shah
3	Paul	Johnson
4	Samuel	Martinez

then the SELECT will return the following data:

CustomerID	FirstName	LastName
1	Sara	Davis
2	Rumi	Shah
3	Paul	Johnson
4	Samuel	Martinez

In other words, it brings back everything in the table.

In the previous chapter, we mentioned that it's a common practice to specify a primary key for all tables. In this example, the CustomerID column is such a column. We also mentioned that primary keys are sometimes set up to automatically generate sequential numbers in a numeric sequence as rows are added to a table. That is the case in this example. In fact, most of the sample data we'll show throughout the book will include a similar column that is both a primary key and defined as auto-increment. By convention, this is generally the first column in a table.

Syntax Notes

Two points must be remembered when writing any SQL statement. First, the keywords in SQL are not case sensitive. The word SELECT is treated identically to "select" or "Select."

Second, a SQL statement can be written on any number of lines and with any number of spaces between words. For example, the SQL statement:

```
SELECT * FROM Customers
```

is identical to:

```
SELECT *
FROM Customers
```

It's usually a good idea to begin each important keyword on a separate line. When we get to more complex SQL statements, this will make it easier to quickly grasp the meaning of the statement.

Finally, as we present different SQL statements in this book, we'll often show both a specific example and a more general format. For instance, the general format of the previous statement would be shown as:

```
SELECT *
FROM table
```

Italics are used to indicate a general expression. The italicized word *table* means that you can substitute any table name in that spot. When you see italicized words in any SQL statement in this book, that is simply a way of indicating that any valid word or phrase can be substituted in that location.

Database Differences: MySQL and Oracle

Many SQL implementations require a semicolon at the end of every statement. This is true of MySQL and Oracle, but not of Microsoft SQL Server. However, semicolons can be specified in SQL Server if desired. For simplicity, we'll show SQL statements without semicolons in this book. If you're using MySQL or Oracle, you'll need to add a semicolon at the end of each statement. The previous statement would appear as:

```
SELECT *
FROM Customers;
```

Comments

When writing SQL statements, it's often desirable to insert comments within or around those statements. There are two standard methods of writing comments in SQL. The first method, referred to as the double dash, consists of two dashes placed anywhere on a line. All text that follows two dashes on that line is ignored and is interpreted as comments. Here's an example of this format:

```
SELECT
-- this is the first comment
FirstName,
LastName -- this is a second comment
FROM Customers
```

The second format, borrowed from the C programming language, consists of text placed between /* and */ characters. Comments between the /* and */ can be written on multiple lines. Here's an example:

```
SELECT
/* this is the first comment */
FirstName,
LastName /* this is a second comment
this is still part of the second comment
this is the end of the second comment */
FROM Customers
```

> **Database Differences: MySQL**
>
> MySQL supports comments in both the double dash and the C programming format (/* and */), with one minor difference. When using the double dash format, MySQL requires a space or special character such as a tab immediately after the second dash.
>
> In addition, MySQL allows for a third method of inserting comments, similar to the double dash. In MySQL, you can place a number sign (#) anywhere on a line to indicate comments. All text after the # symbol on that line is taken as a comment. Here's an example of this format:
>
> ```
> SELECT FirstName
> # this is a comment
> FROM Customers;
> ```

Specifying Columns

So far, we've done nothing more than simply display all the data in a table. But what if we wanted to select only certain columns? Working from the same table, we might want to display only the customer's last name, for example. The SELECT statement would then look like:

```
SELECT LastName
FROM Customers
```

and the resulting data would be:

LastName
Davis
Shah
Johnson
Martinez

If we wanted to select more than one, but not all, columns, the SELECT might look like this:

```
SELECT
FirstName,
LastName
FROM Customers
```

and the output would appear as:

FirstName	LastName
Sara	Davis
Rumi	Shah
Paul	Johnson
Samuel	Martinez

The general format of this statement is:

```
SELECT columnlist
FROM table
```

The important thing to remember is that if you need to specify more than one column in the *columnlist*, then those columns must be separated by a comma. Also notice that we placed each column (FirstName, LastName) in the *columnlist* on separate lines. This was done to improve readability.

Column Names with Embedded Spaces

What if a column contains a space in its name? Say, for example, that the LastName column was specified as Last Name (with a space between the two words). Clearly, the following would not work:

```
SELECT
Last Name
FROM Customers
```

This statement would be considered invalid because Last and Name are not column names, and even if they were proper column names, they would need to be separated by a comma. The solution is to place special characters around any column name containing spaces. The character to use differs, depending on which database you're using. For Microsoft SQL Server, the required characters are square brackets. The syntax is:

```
SELECT
[Last Name]
FROM Customers
```

One additional syntax note: Just as keywords are not case sensitive, it's also true that table and column names are not case sensitive. As such, the previous example is identical to:

```
select
[last name]
from customers
```

For clarity's sake, we'll print all keywords in caps, and we'll also capitalize table and column names in this book, but that is not truly necessary.

Database Differences: MySQL and Oracle

For MySQL, the character to use around column names containing spaces is an accent grave
(`). The MySQL syntax for the above example is:

```
SELECT
`Last Name`
FROM Customers;
```

For Oracle, the character to use around column names containing spaces is the double quote.
The Oracle syntax for the example is:

```
SELECT
"Last Name"
FROM Customers;
```

Additionally, unlike Microsoft SQL Server and MySQL, column names in Oracle surrounded by
double quotes are case sensitive. This means that the previous statement is not equivalent to:

```
SELECT
"LAST NAME"
FROM Customers;
```

Preview of the Full SELECT

The bulk of this book has to do with the SELECT statement introduced in this chapter. In
Chapters 3 through 15, we'll expand on this statement, introducing new features until the full
potential and capabilities of the SELECT are realized and understood. At this point, we have
only introduced this portion of the SELECT statement:

```
SELECT columnlist
FROM table
```

In the interest of removing any remaining suspense, let's look at a preview of the full SELECT
statement and briefly comment on its various components. The full SELECT statement, with all
its clauses is:

```
SELECT columnlist
FROM tablelist
WHERE condition
GROUP BY columnlist
HAVING condition
ORDER BY columnlist
```

We've already been introduced to the SELECT and FROM clauses. Let's expand a bit on those
clauses and talk about the others. The SELECT clause initiates the statement and lists any
columns that will be displayed. As will be seen in later chapters, the *columnlist* can include
not only actual columns from the specified tables, but also calculated columns, usually
derived from one or more columns in the tables. The columns in the *columnlist* can also
include functions, which represent a special way of adding commonly used methods for
transforming data.

The FROM clause specifies the data sources from which data will be drawn. In most cases, these data sources will be tables. In later chapters, we'll learn that these data sources can also be other SELECT statements, which represent a type of virtual *view* of data. In this chapter, our *tablelist* is a single table. One of the key features of SQL to be discussed in later chapters is the ability to combine multiple tables together in a single SELECT statement through something called the JOIN. Thus, we'll see many examples where the *tablelist* in the FROM clause is composed of multiple lines, indicating tables joined together.

The WHERE clause is used to indicate selection logic. This is where you can specify exactly which rows of data are to be retrieved. The WHERE clause can utilize basic arithmetic operators such as equals (=) and greater than (>), along with Boolean operators such as OR and AND.

The GROUP BY clause plays a key role in summarizing data. By organizing data into various groups, the analyst has the ability to not only group data, but to summarize the data in each group through the use of various statistics, such as a sum or count of the data.

When data has been grouped, selection criteria become somewhat more complex. One has to ask whether the selection criteria apply to individual rows or to the entire group. For example, when grouping customers by state, one may only want to see rows of individual customers where the aggregate purchases of all customers in the state exceed a certain amount. This is where the HAVING clause comes in. The HAVING clause is used to specify selection logic for an entire group of data.

Finally, the ORDER BY clause is used to sort the data in an ascending or descending sequence.

As will be made clear in later chapters, the various clauses in a SELECT statement, if they exist, must be specified in the same order shown in the previous general statement. For example, if there is a GROUP BY clause in a SELECT statement, it must appear after a WHERE clause and before a HAVING clause.

In addition to all of the aforementioned clauses, we will also talk about a number of additional ways to organize the SELECT statement, including subqueries and set logic. Subqueries are a way to insert an entire SELECT statement within another SELECT statement, and are often useful for certain types of selection logic. Set logic is a way to combine multiple queries side by side as a single query.

Looking Ahead

In this chapter, we began our exploration of how to use the SELECT statement to retrieve data. We learned about basic syntax and have seen how to select specific columns. In reality, however, this allows us to accomplish very little of a practical nature. Most significantly, we have not yet learned how to apply any type of selection criteria to our data retrieval efforts. For example, while we know how to select all customers, we don't yet know how to select only customers from the state of New York.

As it happens, we won't cover selection criteria until Chapter 6. What will we be doing until then? In the next few chapters, we'll build on what can be done with the *columnlist* component of the SELECT statement. In the following chapter, we'll move on to more variations on column selection, allowing us to create complex calculations in a single column. We'll also talk about ways to rename columns to make them more descriptive. Chapters 4 and 5 will then build on our ability to create even more complex and powerful *columnlists*, so when we finally get to the topic of selection criteria in Chapter 6, we'll have a full arsenal of techniques available at our disposal.

3

Calculated Fields
and Aliases

Keywords Introduced

AS

In the previous chapter, we talked about how to choose individual columns for inclusion in a SELECT statement. We now want to introduce a way to perform calculations on the individual data items retrieved from a database. This technique is referred to as *calculated fields*. Using this approach, customer names can be formatted exactly as desired. Numeric calculations specific to a business or organization can be formulated and presented. In short, SQL developers are often required to customize the content of individual columns in order to successfully turn data into more intelligent information. The inclusion of calculated fields is a useful device that helps to accomplish that goal.

When selecting data from a table, you are not restricted to the columns that happen to be in the table. The concept of calculated fields allows for a number of other possibilities. With calculated fields, you can do the following:

- Display specific words or values
- Perform calculations on single or multiple columns
- Combine columns and specific words or values together

Let's look at a few examples, all coming from this Sales table:

SalesID	FirstName	LastName	QuantityPurchased	PricePerItem
1	Andrew	Li	4	2.50
2	Carol	White	10	1.25
3	James	Carpenter	5	4.00

Literal Values

Our first example of a calculated field isn't really a calculation at all. We're going to select a specific value as a column, even though the value has nothing to do with the data in the table. This type of expression is called a *literal value*. Here's an example:

```
SELECT
'First Name:',
FirstName
FROM Sales
```

This statement will return this data:

(no column name)	FirstName
First Name:	Andrew
First Name:	Carol
First Name:	James

In this statement, we are selecting two data items. The first is the literal value 'First Name: '. Note that single quote marks are used to indicate that this is a literal with character data. The second data item is the FirstName column.

Notice, first, that the literal value 'First Name:' is repeated on every row. Second, there is no header information for the first column. When run in Microsoft SQL Server, the column header displays "(no column name)". The reason why there is no header is simply because this is a calculated field. There is no column name that can be associated with this information.

Database Differences: MySQL and Oracle

Both MySQL and Oracle will return a value in the header row for literal values. In MySQL, the header for the first column in the previous example will appear as:

```
First Name:
```

In Oracle, the header for the first column will appear as:

```
'FIRSTNAME:'
```

One question that might very well be asked is why the header row is important at all. If we're using the SELECT statement only to retrieve some data, then the header itself wouldn't seem to be significant. Only the data itself matters. However, if we're using the SELECT statement to obtain data for a report displayed to a user, either on paper or on a computer screen, then the header might well be relevant. Column headers are normally displayed in a reporting environment. When users look at a column of data in a report, they generally want to know the meaning of the column, and look to the column header for that information. In the case of a literal value, there really is no meaning to the column, so a header isn't truly necessary. But in other types of calculated fields, there may be a meaningful label that could be applied to the column. Later in this chapter, we'll discuss the concept of column aliases, which represent a way of providing a header in this type of situation.

One more point about literals. You might surmise from the previous example that all literals need quotation marks, but that is not necessarily the case. For example, the following statement:

```
SELECT
5,
FirstName
FROM Sales
```

will return this data:

(no column name)	FirstName
5	Andrew
5	Carol
5	James

The literal value 5 is a valid value, even if it's completely meaningless. Because it doesn't have quote marks, the 5 is interpreted as a numeric value.

Arithmetic Calculations

Let's move on to a more typical example of a calculated field. Arithmetic calculations allow us to perform a calculation on one or more columns in a table. For example:

```
SELECT
SalesID,
QuantityPurchased,
PricePerItem,
QuantityPurchased * PricePerItem
FROM Sales
```

This statement will return this data:

SalesID	QuantityPurchased	PricePerItem	(no column name)
1	4	2.50	10.00
2	10	1.25	12.50
3	5	4.00	20.00

As with literals, the fourth column has no header, due to the fact that it isn't derived from a single column. The first three columns of the above SELECT are nothing different from what's been seen previously. The fourth column is a calculated column with this arithmetic expression:

```
QuantityPurchased * PricePerItem
```

In this case, the asterisk symbol denotes multiplication. It doesn't mean "all columns," as was seen in the previous chapter. In addition to the asterisk, several other arithmetic operators are allowed in calculated fields. The most common are:

Arithmetic Operator	Meaning
+	addition
-	subtraction
*	multiplication
/	division

One commonly used arithmetic operator that isn't available in Microsoft SQL Server or MySQL is exponentiation. In order to utilize exponents in SQL, you must use the POWER function. This will be demonstrated in the next chapter.

> **Database Differences: Oracle**
>
> Unlike SQL Server and MySQL, Oracle provides an arithmetic operator for exponentiation. This is denoted by two asterisks (**).

Concatenating Fields

Concatenation is a fancy computer term that means to combine or join character data together. Just as arithmetic operations can be performed on numeric data, character data can be combined, or concatenated, together. The syntax for concatenation varies, depending on the database you're working with. Here's an example from Microsoft SQL Server:

```
SELECT
SalesID,
FirstName,
LastName,
FirstName + ' ' + LastName
FROM Sales
```

The data retrieved is:

SalesID	FirstName	LastName	(no column name)
1	Andrew	Li	Andrew Li
2	Carol	White	Carol White
3	James	Carpenter	James Carpenter

Again, the first three columns are nothing new. The fourth column is derived from this expression in the SQL statement:

```
FirstName + ' ' + LastName
```

The plus sign denotes concatenation. Because the operation involves character rather than numeric data, SQL is smart enough to know that the plus sign means concatenation and not addition. In this case, the concatenation is composed of three terms: the FirstName column, a literal space (' '), and the LastName column. The literal space is necessary so that William Smith doesn't display as WilliamSmith.

Database Differences: MySQL and Oracle

MySQL doesn't use a symbol, such as the plus (+) sign, to denote concatenation. Instead, it requires you to use a function named CONCAT. We'll cover functions in the next chapter, but for now, here is a look at what the same statement looks like in MySQL:

```
SELECT
SalesID,
FirstName,
LastName,
CONCAT(FirstName, ' ', LastName)
FROM Sales;
```

In essence, the CONCAT specifies to combine the three mentioned terms within the parentheses as a single expression.

Oracle uses two vertical bars (||) rather than a plus sign (+) to denote concatenation. The equivalent statement in Oracle is:

```
SELECT
SalesID,
FirstName,
LastName,
FirstName || ' ' || LastName)
FROM Sales;
```

Column Aliases

In all the preceding examples in this chapter, calculated fields were displayed with a nondescriptive (unlabeled) header. Microsoft SQL Server displays "(no column name)" when it encounters a calculated field. We now want to address how a descriptive header can be specified for these types of columns. In brief, the solution is to utilize a column alias. The term *alias* means an alternate name. Here's an example of how to specify a column alias for the previous SELECT statement:

```
SELECT
SalesID,
FirstName,
LastName,
FirstName + ' ' + LastName AS 'Name'
FROM Sales
```

The keyword AS is used to indicate a column alias, which immediately follows the keyword. Notice that the column alias is surrounded by single quotes. The output is:

SalesID	FirstName	LastName	Name
1	Andrew	Li	Andrew Li
2	Carol	White	Carol White
3	James	Carpenter	James Carpenter

The fourth column now has a header. In this example, we placed the column alias within single quotes. These quotes are not strictly necessary, unless the column alias contains embedded spaces. Additionally, the keyword AS isn't necessary. However, we will persist with using the AS keyword in this book to make clear that this is a column alias. Without the single quotes or AS keyword, the previous SELECT statement would be written as follows, with identical results:

```
SELECT
SalesID,
FirstName,
LastName,
FirstName + ' ' + LastName Name
FROM Sales
```

In addition to providing a header for a calculated field, column aliases are often useful when a column in a table has a cryptic name that you'd like to change. For example, if a table has a column with the name "Qty", you could issue this statement to display the column as "Quantity Purchased":

```
SELECT
Qty AS 'Quantity Purchased'
FROM table
```

Database Differences: Oracle

Oracle uses double quotes to delineate column aliases. The previous statement would be written as follows in Oracle:

```
SELECT
SalesID,
FirstName,
LastName,
FirstName || ' ' || LastName AS "Name"
FROM Sales;
```

Table Aliases

In addition to providing alternate names for columns, aliases can also be specified for tables, using the same AS keyword. There are three general reasons for using table aliases. The first reason relates to tables with obscure or complex names. For example, if a table is named Sales123, you can use the following SELECT to give the table an alias of Sales.

```
SELECT,
LastName
FROM Sales123 AS Sales
```

As with column aliases, the AS keyword is optional. However, unlike column aliases, table aliases are not enclosed within quotes. A second reason for using table aliases is to allow you to use that alias name as a prefix for any selected column. For example, the above could also be written as:

```
SELECT,
Sales.LastName
FROM Sales123 AS Sales
```

The word Sales has now been added as a prefix to the LastName column, using a period to separate the prefix from the column name. In this situation, the use of the prefix was strictly optional and somewhat redundant. Because there was only one table in this query, it wasn't necessary to include the table name as a prefix for the column. However, when data is selected from multiple tables, the prefix is often helpful and will sometimes be required. When multiple tables are involved, adding the table name as a prefix helps anyone viewing the query quickly grasp which table each column is from. Furthermore, when a column is named the same in multiple tables, then the use of a table alias is actually required. This usage of column aliases will be illustrated in Chapter 11, "Inner Joins."

A third reason for using table aliases has to do with the use of tables in subqueries. This will be discussed in Chapter 14, "Subqueries."

Database Differences: Oracle

Although the AS keyword can be used for column aliases, Oracle does not permit the AS keyword to denote table aliases. The above SELECT would be written in Oracle as:

```
SELECT
Sales.LastName
FROM Sales123 Sales;
```

Looking Ahead

In this chapter, we discussed three general ways to create calculated fields in a SELECT statement. First, literal values can be used to select specific words or values. Second arithmetic calculations can be applied to one more columns in a single expression. Third, concatenation can be used to combine columns and literal values together. We also discussed the related topic of column aliases, which are often employed when using calculated fields. Finally, we offered a preview of table aliases, a topic that will be covered in greater detail in later chapters.

In the next chapter, we'll move on to the subject of functions, which provide more complex and interesting ways to perform calculations. As mentioned before, we're not quite at the point where we can apply selection criteria to SQL statements. We're still building on the basics of what can be done with the *columnlist* in a SELECT. Your patience with this methodical approach will reap rewards in Chapter 6, when we get to the topic of selection logic.

4

Using Functions

Keywords Introduced

LEFT · RIGHT · SUBSTRING · LTRIM · RTRIM · UPPER · LOWER · GETDATE ·
DATEPART · DATEDIFF · ROUND · PI · POWER · ISNULL

Anyone familiar with Microsoft Excel is probably aware that functions provide a huge amount of functionality for the typical spreadsheet user. Without the ability to use functions, most of the data available in spreadsheets would be of limited value. The same is true in the world of SQL. Familiarity with SQL functions will greatly enhance your ability to generate dynamic results for anyone viewing data or reports generated from SQL.

This chapter covers a wide variety of some of the most commonly used functions in four different categories: character functions, date/time functions, numeric functions, and conversion functions. Additionally, we'll talk about composite functions—a way of combining multiple functions into a single expression.

What Is a Function?

Similar to the calculations covered in the previous chapter, functions provide another way to manipulate data. As was seen, calculations can involve multiple fields, either with arithmetic operators such as multiplication, or by concatenation. Similarly, functions can involve data from multiple values, but the end result of a function is always a single value.

What is a function? A function is merely a rule for transforming any number of input values into one output value. The rule is defined within the function and can't be altered. However, the user of a function is allowed to specify any desired value for the inputs to the function. Some functions may allow some of the inputs to be optional. That means that the specification of that particular input isn't required. Functions can also be designed to have no inputs. However, regardless of the type or number of input values, functions always return precisely one output value when the function is invoked.

There are two types of functions: scalar and aggregate. The term *scalar* comes from mathematics and refers to an operation that is done on a single number. In computer usage, it means that the function is performed on data in a single row. For example, the LTRIM function removes spaces from one specified value in one row of data.

In contrast, aggregate functions are meant to be performed on a larger set of data. For example, the SUM function can be used to calculate the sum of all the values of a specified column. Because aggregate functions apply to larger sets or groups of data, we will leave discussion of this type of function to Chapter 9, "Summarizing Data."

Every SQL database offers dozens of scalar functions. The actual functions vary widely between databases, in terms of both their names and how they work. As a result, we will cover only a few representative examples of some of the more useful functions.

The most common types of scalar functions can be classified under three categories: character, date/time, and numeric. These are functions that allow you to manipulate character, date/time, or numeric datatypes. In addition, we will talk about some useful conversion functions that can be used to convert data from one datatype to another.

Character Functions

Character functions are those that enable you to manipulate character data. Just as character datatypes are sometimes called *string datatypes*, character functions are sometimes called *string functions*. We'll cover these seven examples of character functions: LEFT, RIGHT, SUBSTRING, LTRIM, RTRIM, UPPER, and LOWER.

In this chapter, rather than retrieving data from specific tables, we'll simply use SELECT statements with literal values in the *columnlist*. There will be no FROM clause to indicate a table. Let's start with an example for the LEFT function. When this SQL command is issued:

```
SELECT
LEFT('sunlight',3) AS 'The Answer'
```

this data is returned:

The Answer
sun

The inclusion of a column alias in this SQL statement allows the output to display "The Answer" as a column header. Note that there is no FROM clause in the SELECT statement. Instead of retrieving data from a table, we're selecting data from a single literal value, namely 'sunlight'. In many SQL implementations, including SQL Server and MySQL, a FROM clause isn't strictly necessary in a SELECT statement, although in practice one would seldom write a SELECT statement like this. We're using this format, without a FROM clause, only to more easily illustrate how functions work.

Let's now look at the format of this function in greater detail. The general format of the LEFT function is:

```
LEFT(CharacterValue, NumberOfCharacters)
```

All functions have any number of arguments within the parentheses. For example, the LEFT function has two arguments: *CharacterValue* and *NumberOfCharacters*. The term *argument* is a commonly used mathematical term that describes a component of functions, and has nothing to do with anything being disagreeable or unpleasant. The various arguments that are defined for each function are what truly define the meaning of the function. In the case of the LEFT function, the *CharacterValue* and *NumberOfCharacters* arguments are both needed to define what will happen when the LEFT function is invoked.

The LEFT function has two arguments, and both are required. As mentioned, other functions may have more or fewer arguments. Functions are even permitted to have no arguments. But regardless of the number of arguments, even if zero, all functions have a set of parentheses following the function name. The presence of the parentheses tells you that the expression is a function and not something else.

The formula for the LEFT function says: Take the specified *CharacterValue*, look at the specified *NumberOfCharacters* on the left, and bring back the result. In the previous example, it looks at the CharacterValue 'sunlight' and brings back the left three characters. The result is "sun".

The main point to remember is that for any function you want to use, you'll need to look up the function in the database's reference guide and determine how many arguments are required and what they mean.

The second character function we'll cover is the RIGHT function. This is the same as the LEFT function, except that characters are now specified for the right side of the input value. The general format of the RIGHT function is:

```
RIGHT(CharacterValue, NumberOfCharacters)
```

As an example:

```
SELECT
RIGHT('sunlight',5) AS 'The Answer'
```

returns:

The Answer
light

In this case, the *NumberOfCharacters* argument needed to have a value of 5 in order to return the value "light". A value of 3 would have only returned "ght".

One problem that often arises with the use of the RIGHT function is that character data often contains spaces on the right-hand side. Let's look at an example in which a table with only one row of data contains a column named President, where the column is defined as being 20 characters long. The table looks like:

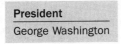

President

George Washington

If we issue this SELECT statement against the table:

```
SELECT
RIGHT(President,10) AS 'Last Name'
FROM table1
```

we get back this data:

Last Name

hington

We expected to get back "Washington" but only got "hington." The problem is that the entire column is 20 characters long. In this example, there are three spaces to the right of the value "George Washington". Therefore, when we ask for the rightmost 10 characters, SQL will take the three spaces, plus another seven characters from the original expression. As will soon be seen, the function RTRIM must be used to remove the ending spaces before using the RIGHT function.

You might be wondering how to select data from the middle of an expression. This is accomplished by using the SUBSTRING function. The general format of that function is:

```
SUBSTRING(CharacterValue, StartingPosition, NumberOfCharacters)
```

For example:

```
SELECT
SUBSTRING('thewhitegoat',4,5) AS 'The Answer'
```

returns this data:

The Answer

white

This function is saying to take five characters, starting with position 4. This results in the display of the word "white".

Database Differences: MySQL and Oracle

MySQL sometimes requires that there be no space between the function name and the left parenthesis. It depends on the specific function used. For example, the previous statement in MySQL must be written exactly as shown. Unlike in Microsoft SQL Server, you can't type in an extra space after SUBSTRING.

In Oracle, the equivalent of the SUBSTRING function is SUBSTR. One difference in the Oracle version of SUBSTR is that the second argument (*StartingPosition*) can have a negative value. A negative value for this argument means that you need to count that number of positions backward from the right side of the column.

As mentioned, Oracle doesn't permit you to write a SELECT statement without a FROM clause. However, Oracle does provide a dummy table called DUAL for this type of situation. The Oracle equivalent of the SELECT with a SUBSTRING function is:

```
SELECT
SUBSTR('thewhitegoat',4,5) AS "The Answer"
FROM DUAL;
```

Our next two character functions enable us to remove all spaces, either on the left or the right side of an expression. The LTRIM function trims characters from the left side of a character expression. For example:

```
SELECT
LTRIM('     the apple') AS 'The Answer'
```

returns this data:

The Answer
the apple

Note that LTRIM is smart enough not to eliminate spaces in the middle of a phrase. It only removes the spaces to the very left of a character value.

Similar to LTRIM, the RTRIM function removes any spaces to the right of a character value. An example of RTRIM will be given in the next section, on composite functions.

The final two character functions to be covered are UPPER and LOWER. These functions convert any word or phrase to upper- or lowercase. The syntax is simple and straightforward. Here's an example that covers both functions:

```
SELECT
UPPER('Abraham Lincoln') AS 'Convert to Uppercase',
        LINCOLN') AS 'Convert to Lowercase'
```

ercase	Convert to Lowercase
COLN	abraham lincoln

Composite Functions

An important characteristic of functions, whether they are character, mathematical, or date/time, is that two or more functions can be combined to create composite functions. A composite function with two functions can be said to be a function of a function. Let's go back to the George Washington query to illustrate. Again, we're working from this data:

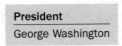

President
George Washington

Remember that the President column is 20 characters long. In other words, there are three spaces to the right of the value "George Washington". In addition to illustrating composite functions, this next example will also cover the RTRIM function mentioned in the previous section. The statement:

```
SELECT
RIGHT(RTRIM (President),10) AS 'Last Name'
FROM table1
```

returns this data:

Last Name
Washington

Why does this now produce the correct value? Let's examine how this composite function works. There are two functions involved: RIGHT and RTRIM. When evaluating composite functions, you always start from the inside and work your way out. In this example, the innermost function is:

```
RTRIM(President)
```

This function takes the value in the President column and eliminates all spaces on the right. After this is done, the RIGHT function is applied to the result to bring back the desired value. Because

```
RTRIM(President)
```

equals "George Washington", we can say that:

```
SELECT
RIGHT(RTRIM (President), 10)
```

is the same as saying:

```
SELECT
RIGHT('George Washington', 10)
```

In other words, we can obtain the desired result by first applying the RTRIM function to the input data and then adding the RIGHT function to the expression to produce the final results.

Date/Time Functions

Date/Time functions allow for the manipulation of date and time values. The names of these functions differ, depending on the database used. In Microsoft SQL Server, the functions we'll cover are called GETDATE, DATEPART, and DATEDIFF.

The simplest of the date/time functions is one that returns the current date and time. In Microsoft SQL Server, the function is named GETDATE. This function has no arguments. It merely returns the current date and time. For example:

```
SELECT GETDATE()
```

brings back an expression with the current date and time. Since the GETDATE function has no arguments, there is nothing specified between the parentheses. Remember that a date/time field is a special datatype that contains both a date and a time in a single field. An example of such a value is:

```
2017-05-15 08:48:30
```

This value refers to the 15th of May 2017, at 48 minutes and 30 seconds past 8 AM.

> ### Database Differences: MySQL and Oracle
>
> In MySQL, the equivalent of GETDATE is NOW. The above statement would be written as:
> ```
> SELECT NOW()
> ```
> The equivalent of GETDATE in Oracle is CURRENT_DATE. The statement is written as:
> ```
> SELECT CURRENT_DATE
> ```

The next date/time function enables us to analyze any specified date and return a value to represent such elements as the day or week of the date. Again, the name of this function differs, depending on the database. In Microsoft SQL Server, this function is called DATEPART. The general format is:

```
DATEPART(DatePart, DateValue)
```

The *DateValue* argument is any date. The *DatePart* argument can have many different values, including year, quarter, month, dayofyear, day, week, weekday, hour, minute, and second.

The following chart shows how the DATEPART function evaluates the date '5/6/2017', with different values for the *DatePart* argument:

DATEPART Function Expression	Resulting Value
DATEPART(month, '5/6/2017')	5
DATEPART(day, '5/6/2017')	6
DATEPART(week, '5/6/2017')	18
DATEPART(weekday, '5/6/2017')	7

Looking at the values in the previous chart, you can see that the month of 5/6/2017 is 5 (May). The day is 2 (Monday). The week is 18, because 5/6/2017 is in the 18th week of the year. The weekday is 7 because 5/6/2017 falls on a Saturday, which is the seventh day of the week.

Database Differences: MySQL and Oracle

In MySQL, the equivalent of the DATEPART function is named DATE_FORMAT, and it utilizes different values for the *DateValue* argument. For example, to return the day of the date '5/6/2017', you would issue this SELECT in MySQL:

```
SELECT DATE_FORMAT('2017-05-06', '%d');
```

Oracle doesn't have a function comparable to DATEPART.

The final date/time function we'll cover, DATEDIFF, enables you to determine quantities such as the number of days between any two dates. The general format is:

```
DATEDIFF (DatePart, StartDate, EndDate)
```

Valid values for the *DatePart* argument for this function include year, quarter, month, dayofyear, day, month, hour, minute, and second. Here's a chart that shows how the DATEDIFF function evaluates the difference between the dates 7/8/2017 and 8/14/2017, with different values for the DatePart argument:

DATEPART Function Expression	Resulting Value
DATEDIFF(day, '7/8/2017', '8/14/2017')	37
DATEDIFF(week, '7/8/2017', '8/14/2017')	6
DATEDIFF(month, '7/8/2017', '8/14/2017')	1
DATEDIFF(year, '7/8/2017', '8/14/2017')	0

The above chart indicates that there are 37 days, or 6 weeks, or 1 month, or 0 years between the two dates.

Database Differences: MySQL and Oracle

In MySQL, the DATEDIFF function only allows you to calculate the number of days between the two dates, and the end date must be listed first to return a positive value. The general format is:

```
DATEDIFF(EndDate, StartDate)
```

Oracle doesn't have a function comparable to DATEDIFF.

Numeric Functions

Numeric functions allow for manipulation of numeric values. Numeric functions are sometimes called *mathematical functions*. The functions we'll cover are ROUND, RAND, PI, and POWER.

The ROUND function allows you to round any numeric value. The general format is:

```
ROUND(NumericValue, DecimalPlaces)
```

The *NumericValue* argument can be any positive or negative number, with or without decimal places, such as 712.863 or –42. The *DecimalPlaces* argument is trickier. It can contain a positive or negative integer, or zero. If *DecimalPlaces* is a positive integer, it means to round to that many decimal places. If *DecimalPlaces* is a negative integer, it means to round to that number of positions to the left of the decimal place. The following chart shows how the number 712.863 is rounded, with different values for the *DecimalPlaces* argument.

ROUND Function Expression	Resulting Value
ROUND(712.863, 3)	712.863
ROUND(712.863, 2)	712.860
ROUND(712.863, 1)	712.900
ROUND(712.863, 0)	713.000
ROUND(712.863, –1)	710.000
ROUND(712.863, –2)	700.000

The PI function merely returns the value of the mathematical number pi. As you may remember from high school geometry, the number pi is an irrational number approximated by the value 3.14. This function is seldom used, but nicely illustrates the point that numeric functions need not have any arguments. For example, the statement:

```
SELECT PI()
```

returns the value 3.14159265358979. To take this example a little further, let's say that we want the value of pi rounded to two decimal places. This can be accomplished by creating a composite function with the PI and ROUND functions. The PI function is used to get the initial value, and the ROUND function is added to round it to two decimal places. The following statement returns a value of 3.14:

```
SELECT ROUND(PI(),2)
```

Database Differences: Oracle

Unlike Microsoft SQL Server and MySQL, Oracle doesn't have a PI function.

The final numeric function we'll cover, which is much more commonly used than PI, is POWER. The POWER function is used to specify a numeric value that includes exponents. The general format of the function is:

```
POWER(NumericValue, Exponent)
```

Let's start with an example that illustrates how to display the number 5 raised to the second power. This is commonly referred to as "5 squared." The SELECT statement:

```
SELECT POWER(5,2) AS '5 Squared'
```

returns this data:

5 Squared
25

In this example, 5 is the numeric value to be evaluated, and 2 is the value of the exponent. Remembering that the square root of a number can be expressed as an exponent with a decimal value less than 1, we can calculate the square root of 25 as follows. The statement:

```
SELECT POWER(25,.5) AS 'Square Root of 25'
```

returns this data:

Square Root of 25
5

In algebraic terms, the calculation takes 25 to the 1/2 (or .5) power. This is the same as taking the square root of 25.

Conversion Functions

All of the aforementioned functions pertain to specific ways to manipulate character, date/time, or numeric datatypes. We now want to address the need to convert data from one datatype to another, or to convert NULL values to something meaningful. The remainder of this chapter will cover two special functions that can be used in these situations.

The CAST function converts data from one datatype to another. The general format of the function is:

```
CAST(Expression AS DataType)
```

The format of this function is slightly different from other functions previously seen, as it uses the word AS to separate the two arguments, rather than a comma. Looking at the usage of the function, it turns out that the CAST function is unnecessary in most situations. Let's take the situation where we want to execute this statement, where the Quantity column is defined as a character datatype:

```
SELECT
2 * Quantity
FROM table
```

Your first impression might be that the statement would fail, due to the fact that Quantity is not defined as a numeric column. However, most SQL databases are smart enough to automatically convert the Quantity column to a numeric value so that it can be multiplied by 2.

Here's an example where the CAST function becomes necessary. Let's say we have dates stored in a column with a character datatype. We'd like to convert those dates to a true date/time column. This statement illustrates how the CAST function can handle that conversion:

```
SELECT
'2017-04-11' AS 'Original Date',
CAST('2017-04-11' AS DATETIME) AS 'Converted Date'
```

The output is:

Original Date	Converted Date
2017-04-11	2017-04-11 00:00:00

The Original Date column looks like a date, but it is really just character data. In contrast, the Converted Date column is a true date/time column, as evidenced by the time value now shown.

A second useful conversion function is one that converts NULL values to a meaningful value. In Microsoft SQL Server, the function is called ISNULL. As mentioned in Chapter 1, "Relational Databases and SQL," NULL values are those for which there is an absence of data. A NULL value is not the same as a space or zero. Let's say we have this table of products:

ProductID	Description	Weight
1	Printer A	NULL
2	Printer B	0
3	Monitor C	2
4	Laptop D	4

Notice that Printer A has a value of NULL in the Weight column. This indicates that a weight for this printer has not yet been provided. Let's say we want to produce a list of all products. When this SELECT is issued:

```
SELECT
Description,
Weight
FROM Products
```

It will show:

Description	Weight
Printer A	NULL
Printer B	0
Monitor C	2
Laptop D	4

There's nothing inaccurate about this display. However, users may prefer to see something such as "Unknown" rather than NULL for missing values. Here's the solution:

```
SELECT
Description,
ISNULL(CAST(Weight AS VARCHAR),'Unknown') AS Weight
FROM Products
```

The following data is displayed:

Description	Weight
Printer A	Unknown
Printer B	0
Monitor C	2
Laptop D	4

Notice that the solution requires the use of both the ISNULL and CAST functions. The ISNULL function handles the display of the weight as "Unknown" when NULL values are encountered. Assuming the Weight column is defined as an integer, the CAST function is needed to convert the weight to a Varchar datatype, so both integer and character values can be displayed in a single column.

Database Differences: MySQL and Oracle

The ISNULL function is called IFNULL in MySQL. Furthermore, MySQL doesn't require the use of the CAST function in this example. The equivalent of the above statement in MySQL is:

```
SELECT
Description,
IFNULL(Weight,'Unknown') AS Weight
FROM Products;
```

The ISNULL function is called NVL (Null Value) in Oracle. The equivalent Oracle statement is:

```
SELECT
Description,
NVL(CAST(Weight AS CHAR),'Unknown') AS Weight
FROM Products;
```

Additionally, unlike Microsoft SQL Server and MySQL, Oracle displays a dash rather than the word NULL when it encounters NULL values.

Looking Ahead

This chapter described a wide variety of functions. Functions are basically predefined rules for transforming a set of values into another value. Just as spreadsheets provide built-in functions for manipulating data, SQL provides similar capabilities. In addition to covering basic character, date/time, numeric, and conversion functions, we also explained how to create composite functions from two or more of these functions.

Because there are simply so many available functions with widely varying possibilities, it's impossible to discuss every nuance of every available function. The thing to remember is that functions can be easily looked up in a database's help system or reference guide when they need to be used. Online reference material will provide details on exactly how each function works and the proper syntax.

In our next chapter, we'll take a break from *columnlist* issues and talk about something a little more interesting: how to sort data. Sorts can serve lots of useful purposes and satisfy the basic desire of users to view data in some type of order. With the sort, we will begin to think of the entire way in which information is presented, rather than with just bits and pieces of individual data items.

5

Sorting Data

Keywords Introduced

ORDER BY · ASC · DESC

The ability to present data in a sorted order is often essential to the task at hand. For example, if an analyst is shown a large list of customers in a random order, they'd probably find it difficult to locate one particular customer. However, if the same list is sorted alphabetically, the desired customer can quickly be located.

The idea of sorting data applies to many situations, even when the data isn't alphabetic in nature. For example, orders can be sorted by order date, allowing one to rapidly find an order taken at a particular date and time. Alternatively, orders can be sorted by the order amount, allowing orders to be viewed from the smallest to largest. No matter what particular form a sort takes, it can add a useful way of organizing the data being presented to an end user.

Sorting in Ascending Order

Up until now, data has not been returned in any particular order. When a SELECT is issued, you never know which row will come first. If the query is executed from within a software program, and no one ever sees the data at that point in time, then it really doesn't matter. But if the data is to be immediately displayed to a user, then the order of rows is often significant. A sort can be easily added to a SELECT statement by using an ORDER BY clause.

Here's the general format for a SELECT statement with an ORDER BY clause:

```
SELECT columnlist
FROM tablelist
ORDER BY columnlist
```

The ORDER BY clause is always placed after the FROM clause, which in turn always comes after the SELECT keyword. The italicized *columnlist* for the SELECT and ORDER BY keywords indicates that any number of columns can be listed. The columns in *columnlist* can be individual columns or more complex expressions. Also, the columns specified after the SELECT and ORDER BY keywords can be entirely different columns. The italicized *tablelist* indicates that any number of tables can be listed in the FROM clause. The syntax for listing multiple tables will be introduced in Chapter 11, "Inner Joins," and Chapter 12, "Outer Joins."

For the following few examples on sorting, we'll work from data in this Salespeople table:

SalespersonID	FirstName	LastName
1	Gregory	Brown
2	Carla	Brown
3	Natalie	Lopez
4	Connie	King

To sort data in an alphabetic order, with A coming before Z, we simply need to add an ORDER BY clause to the SELECT statement. For example:

```
SELECT
FirstName,
LastName
FROM Salespeople
ORDER BY LastName
```

brings back this data:

FirstName	LastName
Gregory	Brown
Carla	Brown
Natalie	Lopez
Connie	King

Because there are two Browns, Carla and Gregory, there's no way to predict which one will be listed first. This is because we are sorting only on LastName, and there are multiple rows with that same last name.

Similarly, if we issue this SELECT:

```
SELECT
FirstName,
LastName
FROM Salespeople
ORDER BY FirstName
```

then this data is retrieved:

FirstName	LastName
Carla	Brown
Connie	King
Gregory	Brown
Natalie	Lopez

The order is now completely different, because the sort is by first name rather than last name.

SQL provides a special keyword named ASC, which stands for *ascending*. This keyword is completely optional and largely unnecessary, because all sorts are assumed to be in ascending order by default. The following SELECT, which uses the ASC keyword, returns the same data shown previously.

```
SELECT
FirstName,
LastName
FROM Salespeople
ORDER BY FirstName ASC
```

In essence, the keyword ASC can be used to emphasize the fact that the sort is in ascending, rather than descending, order.

Sorting in Descending Order

The DESC keyword sorts in an order opposite to ASC. Instead of ascending, the order in such a sort is descending. For example:

```
SELECT
FirstName,
LastName
FROM Salespeople
ORDER BY FirstName DESC
```

retrieves:

FirstName	LastName
Natalie	Lopez
Gregory	Brown
Connie	King
Carla	Brown

The first names are now in a Z-to-A order.

Sorting by Multiple Columns

We now return to the problem of what to do with the Browns. To sort by last name when there is more than one person with the same last name, we must add a secondary sort by first name, as follows:

```
SELECT
FirstName,
LastName
FROM Salespeople
ORDER BY LastName, FirstName
```

This brings back:

FirstName	LastName
Carla	Brown
Gregory	Brown
Connie	King
Natalie	Lopez

Because a second sort column is now specified, we can now be certain that Carla Brown will appear before Gregory Brown. Note that LastName must be listed before FirstName in the ORDER BY clause. The order of the columns is significant. The first column listed always has the primary sort value. Any additional columns listed become secondary, tertiary, and so on.

Sorting by a Calculated Field

We'll now apply our knowledge of calculated fields and aliases from Chapter 3 to illustrate some further possibilities for sorts. This statement:

```
SELECT
LastName + ', ' + FirstName AS 'Name'
FROM Salespeople
ORDER BY Name
```

returns this data:

Name
Brown, Carla
Brown, Gregory
King, Connie
Lopez, Natalie

As seen, we utilized concatenation to create a calculated field with an alias of Name. We are able to refer to that same column alias in the ORDER BY clause. This nicely illustrates another benefit of using column aliases. Also, note the design of the calculated field itself. We inserted a column and a space between the last name and first name columns to separate them, and to show the name in a commonly used format. Conveniently, this format also works well for sorting. The ability to display names in this format, with a comma separating the last and first name, is a handy trick to keep in mind. Users very often want to see names arranged in this manner.

It's also possible to put a calculated field in the ORDER BY clause without also using it as a column alias. Similar to the above, we could also specify:

```
SELECT
FirstName,
LastName
FROM Salespeople
ORDER BY LastName + FirstName
```

This would display:

FirstName	LastName
Carla	Brown
Gregory	Brown
Connie	King
Natalie	Lopez

The data is sorted the same as in the prior example. The only difference is that we're now specifying a calculated field in the ORDER BY clause without making use of column aliases. This gives the same result as if LastName and FirstName were specified as the primary and secondary sort columns.

Sort Sequences

In the previous examples, all of the data is character data, consisting of letters from A to Z. There are no numbers or special characters. Additionally, there has been no consideration of upper- and lowercase letters.

Every database lets users specify or customize collation settings that provide details on how data is sorted. The settings vary among databases, but three facts are generally true. First, when data is sorted in an ascending order, any data with NULL values appear first. As previously discussed, NULL values are those where there is an absence of data. After any NULLs, numbers will appear before characters. For data sorted in descending order, character data will display first, then numbers, and then NULLs.

Second, for character data, there is usually no differentiation between upper- and lowercase. An e is the treated the same as an E. Third, for character data, the individual characters that make up the value are evaluated from left to right. If we're talking about letters, then AB will come before AC. Let's look at an example, taken from this table, which we'll refer to as TableForSort:

TableID	CharacterData	NumericData
1	23	23
2	5	5
3	Dog	NULL
4	NULL	–6

In this table, the CharacterData column is defined as a character column, for example as VARCHAR (a variable length datatype). Similarly, the NumericData column is defined as a numeric column, such as INT (an integer datatype). Values with no data are displayed as NULL. When this SELECT is issued against the TableForSort table:

```
SELECT
NumericData
FROM TableForSort
ORDER BY NumericData
```

it will display:

NumericData
NULL
–6
5
23

Notice that NULLs come first, then the numbers in numeric sequence. If we want the NULL values to assume a default value of 0, we can use the ISNULL function discussed in the previous chapter and issue this SELECT statement:

```
SELECT
ISNULL(NumericData,0) AS 'NumericData'
FROM TableForSort
ORDER BY ISNULL(NumericData,0)
```

The result is now:

NumericData
–6
0
5
23

The ISNULL function converted the NULL value to a 0, which results in a different sort order.

The decision as to whether to display NULL values as NULL or as 0 depends on the specific circumstance. If the user thinks of NULL values as meaning 0, then they should be displayed as 0. However, if the user sees NULL values as an absence of data, then displaying the word NULL is appropriate.

Turning to a different ORDER BY clause against the same table, if we issue this SELECT:

```
SELECT
CharacterData
FROM TableForSort
ORDER BY CharacterData
```

it will display:

CharacterData
NULL
23
5
Dog

As expected, NULLs come first, then values with numeric digits, and then values with alphabetic characters. Notice that 23 comes before 5. This is because the 23 and 5 values are being evaluated as characters, not as numbers. Because character data is evaluated from left to right and 2 is lower than 5, 23 is displayed first.

Looking Ahead

In this chapter, we talked about the basic possibilities for sorting data in a specific order. We illustrated how to sort by more than one column. We also discussed the use of calculated fields in sorts. Finally, we covered some of the quirks of sorting, particularly when it comes to data with NULL values and with numbers in character columns.

At the beginning of the chapter, we mentioned some of the general uses for sorts. Primary among these is the ability to simply place data in an easily understood order, thus allowing users to quickly locate a desired piece of information. People generally like to see data in some kind of order, and sorts accomplish that goal. Another interesting use of sorts will be covered in Chapter 6, "Selection Criteria." In that chapter, we'll introduce the keyword TOP and another way to use sorts in conjunction with that keyword. This technique, commonly known as a Top N sort, allows us to do such things as display customers with the five highest orders for a given time period.

In our next chapter, we'll move beyond our analysis of what can be done with *columnlists* and discuss data selection. The ability to specify selection criteria in SELECT statements is critical to most normal queries. In the real world, it would be very unusual to issue a SELECT statement without some sort of selection criteria. The topics discussed in the next chapter address this important topic.

6

Selection Criteria

Keywords Introduced

WHERE · TOP · LIKE

Up until this point, the SELECT statements we've seen have always brought back every row in the table. This would rarely be the case in real-world situations. One is normally interested only in retrieving data that meets certain criteria. For example, if you're selecting orders, you probably only want to see orders that meet certain conditions. When looking at products, you ordinarily only want to view certain types of products. Rarely does someone want to simply see everything. Your interest in data is typically directed toward a small subset of that data in order to analyze or view one particular aspect.

Applying Selection Criteria

Selection criteria in SQL begins with the WHERE clause. The WHERE keyword accomplishes the task of selecting a subset of rows. This is the general format of the SELECT statement, including the WHERE clause and other clauses previously discussed:

```
SELECT columnlist
FROM tablelist
WHERE condition
ORDER BY columnlist
```

As can be seen, the WHERE clause must always come between the FROM and ORDER BY clauses. In fact, if any clause is used, it must appear in the order shown above.

Let's look at an example, taken from data in this Sales table:

SalesID	FirstName	LastName	QuantityPurchased	PricePerItem
1	Andrew	Li	4	2.50
2	Carol	White	10	1.25
3	James	Carpenter	5	4.00

We'll start with a statement with a simple WHERE clause:

```
SELECT
FirstName,
LastName,
QuantityPurchased
FROM Sales
WHERE LastName = 'Carpenter'
```

The output is:

FirstName	LastName	QuantityPurchased
James	Carpenter	5

Because the WHERE clause stipulates to select only rows with a LastName equal to 'Carpenter', only one of the three rows in the table is returned. Notice that the desired value of the LastName column was enclosed in quotes, due to the fact that LastName is a character column. For numeric fields, no quotes are necessary. For example, the following SELECT is equally valid and returns the same data:

```
SELECT
FirstName,
LastName,
QuantityPurchased
FROM Sales
WHERE QuantityPurchased = 5
```

WHERE Clause Operators

In the previous statements, an equals sign (=) is used as the operator in the WHERE clause. The equals sign indicates a test for equality. The general format shown above requires that a *condition* follows the WHERE clause. This condition consists of an operator with expressions on either side.

The following is a list of the basic operators that can be used in the WHERE clause:

WHERE Operator	Meaning
=	equals
<>	does not equal
>	is greater than
<	is less than
>=	is greater than or equal to
<=	is less than or equal to

More advanced operators will be covered in the next chapter.

The meaning of the equals (=) and does not equal (<>) operators should be obvious. Here's an example of a WHERE clause with an "is greater than" operator, taken from the same Sales table:

```
SELECT
FirstName,
LastName,
QuantityPurchased
FROM Sales
WHERE QuantityPurchased > 6
```

The result is:

FirstName	LastName	QuantityPurchased
Carol	White	10

In this example, only one row meets the condition that the QuantityPurchased column be greater than 6. Although not as commonly used, it is also possible to use the "is greater than" operator with a text column. This example:

```
SELECT
FirstName,
LastName
FROM Sales
WHERE LastName > 'K'
```

returns:

FirstName	LastName
Andrew	Li
Carol	White

Because the test is for last names greater than K, it brings back only Li and White, but not Carpenter. When applied to text fields, the greater than and less than operators indicate selection by the alphabetic order of the values. In this case, Li and White are returned, since L and W come after K in the alphabet.

Limiting Rows

We may sometimes want to select a small subset of the rows in a table, but don't care which rows are returned. Let's say we have a table with 50,000 rows and want to see just a few rows of data to see what it looks like. It wouldn't make sense to use the WHERE clause for this purpose, since we don't care which particular rows are returned.

For this situation, the solution is to use a special keyword to specify a limit as to how many rows are returned. This is another instance where syntax differs among databases. In Microsoft SQL Server, the keyword that accomplishes this limit is TOP. The general format is:

```
SELECT
TOP number columnlist
FROM tablelist
```

Database Differences: MySQL and Oracle

MySQL uses the keyword LIMIT rather than TOP. The general format is:

```
SELECT columnlist
FROM tablelist
LIMIT number
```

Oracle uses the keyword ROWNUM rather than TOP. The ROWNUM keyword must be specified in a WHERE clause, as follows:

```
SELECT columnlist
FROM tablelist
WHERE ROWNUM <= number
```

Let's say that we want to see the first 10 rows from a table. The SELECT to accomplish this looks like:

```
SELECT
TOP 10 *
FROM table
```

This statement returns all columns in the first 10 rows from the table. Like any SELECT statement without an ORDER BY clause, there's no way to predict which 10 rows will be returned. It depends on how the data is physically stored in the table.

Similarly, we can list specific columns to return:

```
SELECT
TOP 10
column1,
column2
FROM table
```

In essence, the TOP keyword accomplishes something similar to the WHERE clause, as it returns a small subset of rows in the specified table. However, keep in mind that rows returned using the TOP keyword are not a true random sample, in a statistical sense. They're only the first rows that qualify, based on how the data is physically stored in the database.

Limiting Rows with a Sort

Another use of the TOP keyword is to use it in combination with the ORDER BY clause to obtain a designated number of rows with the highest values, based on specified criteria. This type of data selection is commonly referred to as a *Top N* selection. Here's an example, taken from this Books table:

BookID	Title	Author	CurrentMonthSales
1	Pride and Prejudice	Austen	15
2	Animal Farm	Orwell	7
3	Merchant of Venice	Shakespeare	5
4	Romeo and Juliet	Shakespeare	8
5	Oliver Twist	Dickens	3
6	Candide	Voltaire	9
7	The Scarlet Letter	Hawthorne	12
8	Hamlet	Shakespeare	2

Let's say we want to see the three books that sold the most in the current month. The SELECT that accomplishes this is:

```
SELECT
TOP 3
Title AS 'Book Title',
CurrentMonthSales AS 'Quantity Sold'
FROM Books
ORDER BY CurrentMonthSales DESC
```

The output is:

Book Title	Quantity Sold
Pride and Prejudice	15
The Scarlet Letter	12
Candide	9

Let's examine this statement in some detail. The TOP 3 in the second line indicates that only three rows of data are to be returned. The main question to ask is how it determines which three rows to display. The answer is found in the ORDER BY clause. If there were no ORDER BY clause, then the SELECT would simply bring back any three rows of data. However, this is not what we want. We're looking for the three rows with the highest sales. To accomplish this, we need to sort the rows by the CurrentMonthSales column in descending order. Why descending? When data is sorted in descending order, the highest numbers appear first. If we had sorted in an ascending order, we would get the books with the least number of sales, not the most.

Let's now add one more twist to this scenario. Let's say we only want to see which book by Shakespeare has sold the most. In order to accomplish this, we need to add a WHERE clause, as follows:

```
SELECT
TOP 1
Title AS 'Book Title',
CurrentMonthSales AS 'Quantity Sold'
FROM Books
WHERE Author = 'Shakespeare'
ORDER BY CurrentMonthSales DESC
```

This brings back this data:

Book Title	Quantity Sold
Romeo and Juliet	8

The WHERE clause adds the qualification to look only at books by Shakespeare. We also revised the TOP keyword to specify TOP 1, indicating that we want to see only one row of data.

Pattern Matching

We now want to turn to a situation in which the data to be retrieved is not precisely defined. We often want to view data based on inexact matches with words or phrases. For example, you might be interested in finding companies whose name contains the word "bank." The selection of data via inexact matches within phrases is often referred to as *pattern matching*. In SQL, the LIKE operator is used in the WHERE clause to enable us to find matches against part of a column value. The LIKE operator requires the use of special wildcard characters to specify exactly how the match should work. Let's start with an example from the following Movies table.

MovieID	MovieTitle	Rating
1	Love Actually	R
2	North by Northwest	Not Rated
3	Love and Death	PG
4	The Truman Show	PG
5	Everyone Says I Love You	R
6	Down with Love	PG-13
7	Finding Nemo	G

Our first example with a LIKE operator is:

```
SELECT
MovieTitle AS 'Movie'
FROM Movies
WHERE MovieTitle LIKE '%LOVE%'
```

In this example, the percent (%) sign is used as a wildcard. The percent (%) wildcard means *any characters*. *Any characters* includes the possibility of there being no characters. The percent (%) before LOVE means that we will accept a phrase with any (or no) characters before LOVE. Similarly, the percent (%) after LOVE means that we'll accept a phrase with any (or no) characters after LOVE. In other words, we're looking for any movie title that contains the word LOVE. Here is the data returned from the SELECT:

Movie
Love Actually
Love and Death
Everyone Says I Love You
Down with Love

Notice that LOVE appears as the first word, the last word, and sometimes in the middle of the movie title.

Database Differences: Oracle

Unlike Microsoft SQL Server and MySQL, Oracle is case sensitive when determining matches for literal values. In Oracle, LOVE is not the same as Love. An equivalent statement in Oracle is:

```
SELECT
MovieTitle AS Movie
FROM Movies
WHERE MovieTitle LIKE '%LOVE%';
```

This would return no data, because no movie title contains the word LOVE in all uppercase. One solution in Oracle is to use the UPPER function to convert your data to uppercase, as follows:

```
SELECT
MovieTitle AS Movie
FROM Movies
WHERE UPPER(MovieTitle) LIKE '%LOVE%';
```

Let's now attempt to find only movies that begin with LOVE. If we issue:

```
SELECT
MovieTitle AS 'Movie'
FROM Movies
WHERE MovieTitle LIKE 'LOVE%'
```

we will retrieve only this data:

Movie
Love Actually
Love and Death

Because we're now specifying the percent (%) wildcard only after the word LOVE, we get back only movies that begin with LOVE. Similarly, if we issue:

```
SELECT
MovieTitle AS 'Movie'
FROM Movies
WHERE MovieTitle LIKE '%LOVE'
```

we get only this data:

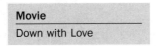

Movie
Down with Love

This is because we have now specified that the phrase must *end* with the word LOVE.

One might ask how to arrange the wildcards to see only movies that contain the word LOVE in the middle of the title, without seeing movies where LOVE is at the beginning or end. The solution is to specify:

```
SELECT
MovieTitle AS 'Movie'
FROM Movies
WHERE MovieTitle LIKE '% LOVE %'
```

Notice that a space has been inserted between the word LOVE and the percent (%) wildcards on either side. This ensures that there is at least one space on both sides of the word. The data brought back from this statement is:

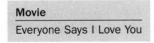

Movie
Everyone Says I Love You

Wildcards

The percent (%) sign is the most common wildcard used with the LIKE operator, but there are a few other possibilities. These include the underscore character (_), a *characterlist* enclosed in square brackets, and a caret symbol (^) plus a *characterlist* enclosed in square brackets. The following table lists these wildcards and their meanings:

Wildcard	Meaning
%	any characters (can be zero characters)
_	exactly one character (can be any character)
[*characterlist*]	exactly one character in the *characterlist*
[^*characterlist*]	exactly one character *not* in the *characterlist*

We'll use the following Actors table to illustrate statements for these wildcards.

ActorID	FirstName	LastName
1	Cary	Grant
2	Mary	Steenburgen
3	Jon	Voight
4	Dustin	Hoffman
5	John	Wayne
6	Gary	Cooper

Here's an illustration of how the underscore (_) wildcard character can be used:

```
SELECT
FirstName,
LastName
FROM Actors
WHERE FirstName LIKE '_ARY'
```

The output of this SELECT is:

FirstName	LastName
Cary	Grant
Mary	Steenburgen
Gary	Cooper

This statement retrieves these three actors because all have a first name consisting of exactly one character followed by the phrase ARY.

Likewise, if we issue this statement:

```
SELECT
FirstName,
LastName
FROM Actors
WHERE FirstName LIKE 'J_N'
```

it produces:

FirstName	LastName
Jon	Voight

The actor John Wayne is not selected since John doesn't fit the J_N pattern. An underscore stands for only one character.

The final wildcards we'll discuss, [*characterlist*] and [^*characterlist*], enable you to specify multiple wildcard values in a single position.

> ### Database Differences: MySQL and Oracle
> The [*characterlist*] and [^*characterlist*] wildcards are not available in MySQL or Oracle.

The following illustrates the [*characterlist*] wildcard:

```
SELECT
FirstName,
LastName
FROM Actors
WHERE FirstName LIKE '[CM]ARY'
```

This retrieves any rows where FirstName begins with a C or M and ends with ARY. The result is:

FirstName	LastName
Cary	Grant
Mary	Steenburgen

The following illustrates the [^*characterlist*] wildcard:

```
SELECT
FirstName,
LastName
FROM Actors
WHERE FirstName LIKE '[^CM]ARY'
```

This selects any rows where FirstName does not begin with a C or M and ends with ARY. The result is:

FirstName	LastName
Gary	Cooper

Looking Ahead

This chapter introduced the topic of how to apply selection criteria to queries. A number of basic operators, such as equals and greater than, were introduced. The ability to specify these types of basic selection criteria goes a long way toward making the SELECT statement truly useful. We also covered the related topic of limiting the number of rows returned in a query. The ability to limit rows in combination with an ORDER BY clause allows for a useful Top N type of data selection.

We concluded the chapter with a study of matching words or phrases via a specified pattern. Matching by patterns is a significant and widely used function of SQL. Any time you enter a word in a search box and attempt to retrieve all entities containing that word, you are utilizing pattern matching.

In our next chapter, "Boolean Logic," we'll greatly enhance our selection criteria capabilities by introducing a number of new keywords that add sophisticated logic to the WHERE clause. At present, we can do such things as select all customers from the state of New York. In the real world, however, much more is typically required. Boolean logic will allow us to formulate a query that will select customers who are in New York or California but not in Los Angeles or Albuquerque.

7

Boolean Logic

Keywords Introduced

AND · OR · NOT · BETWEEN · IN · IS NULL

We introduced the concept of selection criteria in the previous chapter, but only in its simplest form. We'll now expand on that concept to greatly enhance our ability to specify the rows returned from a SELECT. This is where the pure logic of SQL comes into play. In this chapter, we'll introduce a number of operators that will allow you to create complex logical expressions.

Given these new capabilities, if a user comes to you and requests a list of all female customers who live in zip codes 60601 through 62999 but excluding anyone under the age of 30 or who doesn't have an email address, that will be something you can provide.

Complex Logical Conditions

The WHERE clause introduced in the previous chapter used only simple selection criteria. We saw clauses such as:

```
WHERE QuantityPurchased = 5
```

The condition expressed in this WHERE clause is quite basic. It specifies merely to return all rows where the QuantityPurchased column has a value of 5. In the real world, the selection of data is often far from this straightforward. Accordingly, let's now turn our attention to methods of specifying some more complex logical conditions in selection criteria.

The ability to devise complex logical conditions is sometimes called *Boolean logic*. This term, taken from mathematics, refers to the ability to formulate complex conditions that are evaluated as either true or false. In the aforementioned example, the condition QuantityPurchased = 5 is evaluated as either true or false for each row in the table. Obviously, we want to see only rows where the condition is evaluated as true.

The principle keywords used to create complex Boolean logic are AND, OR, and NOT. These three operators are used to provide additional functionality to the WHERE clause. In proper combination, the AND, OR, and NOT operators, along with parentheses, can specify just about any logical expression that can be imagined.

The AND Operator

The following examples will all be taken from this Purchases table:

PurchaseID	CustomerName	State	QuantityPurchased	PricePerItem
1	Andrew Li	IL	4	2.50
2	Carol White	CA	10	1.25
3	James Carpenter	NY	5	4.00

Here's an example of a WHERE clause that uses the AND operator:

```
SELECT
CustomerName,
QuantityPurchased
FROM Purchases
WHERE QuantityPurchased > 3
AND QuantityPurchased < 7
```

The AND clause means that all conditions must evaluate to true for the row to be selected. This SELECT specifies that the only rows to be retrieved are those for which the QuantityPurchased is both greater than 3 and less than 7. Therefore, only these two rows are returned:

CustomerName	QuantityPurchased
Andrew Li	4
James Carpenter	5

Notice that the row for Carol White is not returned. Why? Carol purchased a quantity of 10, which, in fact, does satisfy the first condition (QuantityPurchased > 3). However, the second condition (QuantityPurchased < 7) is not satisfied and therefore is not true. When using the AND operator, all conditions specified must be true for the row to be selected.

The OR Operator

Now let's look at the OR operator. The AND operator meant that all conditions must evaluate to true for the row to be selected. The OR operator means that the row will be selected if *any* of the conditions are determined to be true.

Here's an example, taken from the same table:

```
SELECT
CustomerName,
QuantityPurchased,
PricePerItem
FROM Purchases
WHERE QuantityPurchased > 8
OR PricePerItem > 3
```

This SELECT returns this data:

CustomerName	QuantityPurchased	PricePerItem
Carol White	10	1.25
James Carpenter	5	4.00

Why are the rows for Carol White and James Carpenter displayed, and not the row for Andrew Li? The row for Carol White is selected because it meets the requirements of the first condition (QuantityPurchased > 8). It doesn't matter that the second condition (PricePerItem > 3) isn't true, because only one condition needs to be true for an OR condition.

Likewise, the row for James Carpenter is selected because the second condition (PricePerItem > 3) is true for that row. The row for Andrew Li isn't selected because it doesn't satisfy either of the two conditions.

Using Parentheses

Let's say that we are interested only in orders from customers from either the state of Illinois or the state of California. Additionally, we want to see orders only where the quantity purchased is greater than 8. To attempt to satisfy this request, we might put together this SELECT statement:

```
SELECT
CustomerName,
State,
QuantityPurchased
FROM Purchases
WHERE State = 'IL'
OR State = 'CA'
AND QuantityPurchased > 8
```

We would expect this statement to return only one row of data, for Carol White. Although we have two rows for customers in Illinois or California (Li and White), only one of those (White) has a quantity purchased greater than 8. However, when this statement is executed, we get:

CustomerName	State	QuantityPurchased
Andrew Li	IL	4
Carol White	CA	10

We see two rows instead of the expected one. What went wrong? The answer lies in how SQL interprets the WHERE clause, which happens to contain both AND and OR operators. Like other computer languages, SQL has a predetermined order of evaluation that specifies the order in which various operators are interpreted. Unless told otherwise, SQL always processes the AND operator before the OR operator. So, in the previous statement, it first looks at the AND, and evaluates the condition:

```
State = 'CA'
AND QuantityPurchased > 8
```

The row that satisfies that condition is for Carol White. SQL then evaluates the OR operator, which allows for rows where the State equals IL. That adds the row for Andrew Li. The result is that SQL determines that both the Andrew Li and the Carol White rows meet the condition.

Obviously, this isn't what was intended. This type of problem often comes up when AND and OR operators are combined in a single WHERE clause. The way to resolve the ambiguity is to use parentheses to specify the desired order of evaluation. Anything in parentheses is always evaluated first.

Here's how parentheses can be added to the previous SELECT to correct the situation:

```
SELECT
CustomerName,
State,
QuantityPurchased
FROM Purchases
WHERE (State = 'IL'
OR State = 'CA')
AND QuantityPurchased > 8
```

When this is executed, we see this data:

CustomerName	State	QuantityPurchased
Carol White	CA	10

The parentheses in the SELECT statement force the OR expression (State = 'IL' OR State = 'CA') to be evaluated first. This produces the intended result.

Multiple Sets of Parentheses

Let's say we want to select two different sets of rows from the Purchases table: first, rows for customers in New York, and second, rows for customers in Illinois who have made a purchase with a quantity between 3 and 10. The following SELECT accomplishes this requirement:

```
SELECT
CustomerName,
State,
QuantityPurchased
FROM Purchases
WHERE State = 'NY'
OR (State = 'IL'
AND (QuantityPurchased >= 3
AND QuantityPurchased <= 10))
```

The result is:

CustomerName	State	QuantityPurchased
Andrew Li	IL	4
James Carpenter	NY	5

Notice that there are two sets of parentheses in this statement, with one set inside the other. This use of parentheses is analogous to the parentheses used in the composite functions seen in Chapter 4. When there is more than one set of parentheses, the innermost set of functions is always evaluated first. The same is true of parentheses used in Boolean expressions. In this example, the innermost set of parentheses contains:

```
(QuantityPurchased >= 3
AND QuantityPurchased <= 10)
```

After this condition is evaluated for each row, the logic proceeds outward to the second set of parentheses:

```
(State = 'IL'
AND (QuantityPurchased >= 3
AND QuantityPurchased <= 10))
```

Finally, the logic adds in the final line of the WHERE clause (not enclosed in any parentheses) regarding the state of New York:

```
WHERE State = 'NY'
OR (State = 'IL'
AND (QuantityPurchased >= 3
AND QuantityPurchased <= 10))
```

In essence, SQL's logic first evaluated expressions in the innermost set of parentheses, then the outer set of parentheses, and then all remaining expressions.

The NOT Operator

In addition to the AND and OR operators, the NOT operator is often useful for expressing a complex logical condition. The NOT expresses a negation, or opposite, of whatever follows the NOT. Here's a simple example:

```
SELECT
CustomerName,
State,
QuantityPurchased
FROM Purchases
WHERE NOT State = 'NY'
```

The result is:

CustomerName	State	QuantityPurchased
Andrew Li	IL	4
Carol White	CA	10

This specifies a selection of rows for which the state is not equal to NY. In this simple case, the NOT operator is not truly necessary. The logic of the previous statement can also be accomplished via the following equivalent statement:

```
SELECT
CustomerName,
State,
QuantityPurchased
FROM Purchases
WHERE State <> 'NY'
```

Here, the not equals operator (<>) accomplishes the same thing as the NOT operator. Here's a more complex example with the NOT operator:

```
SELECT
CustomerName,
State,
QuantityPurchased
FROM Purchases
WHERE NOT (State = 'IL'
OR State = 'NY')
```

The result is:

CustomerName	State	QuantityPurchased
Carol White	CA	10

When the NOT operator is used before a set of parentheses, it negates everything in the parentheses. In this example, we're looking for all rows for which the state is *not* Illinois or New York.

Again, note that the NOT operator is not strictly necessary in this example. The logic of the previous query can also be accomplished with the following equivalent statement:

```
SELECT
CustomerName,
State,
QuantityPurchased
FROM Purchases
WHERE State <> 'IL'
AND State <> 'NY'
```

It might take a bit of reflection to understand why the preceding two statements are equivalent. The first statement uses the NOT operator and a logical expression with an OR operator. The second statement converts the logic into an expression with an AND operator.

Here's a final example of how the NOT operator can be used in a complex statement:

```
SELECT
CustomerName,
State,
QuantityPurchased
FROM Purchases
WHERE NOT (State = 'IL'
AND QuantityPurchased > 3)
```

This query is saying to select customers where it's not true that the state equals Illinois and has a QuantityPurchased greater than 3. The NOT operator applies to the entire logical expression that the state equals Illinois and has a QuantityPurchased greater than 3. The result is:

CustomerName	State	QuantityPurchased
Carol White	CA	10
James Carpenter	NY	5

These two rows were selected because the only customer in Illinois who also has a QuantityPurchased greater than 3 is Andrew Li. Because we're applying a NOT to this entire logic, the end result is the display of the other two customers.

Once again, this query can be expressed in an alternate way without using the NOT:

```
SELECT
CustomerName,
State,
QuantityPurchased
FROM Purchases
WHERE State <> 'IL'
OR QuantityPurchased <= 3
```

As seen in these examples, it may not be logically necessary to use the NOT operator in complex expressions with arithmetic operators such as equals (=) or less than (<). However, it's often more straightforward to place a NOT in front of a logical expression rather than attempting to convert that expression into one that doesn't use the NOT. In other words, the NOT operator can provide a convenient and useful way of expressing one's logical thoughts.

The BETWEEN Operator

Let's now turn to two special operators, BETWEEN and IN, that can simplify expressions that would ordinarily require the OR or AND operators. The BETWEEN operator allows us to abbreviate an AND expression with greater than or equal to (>=) and less than or equal to (<=) operators in an expression with a single operator.

Here's an example. Let's say we want to select all rows with a quantity purchased from 5 to 20. One way of accomplishing this is with the following SELECT statement:

```
SELECT
CustomerName,
QuantityPurchased
FROM Purchases
WHERE QuantityPurchased >= 5
AND QuantityPurchased <= 20
```

Using the BETWEEN operator, the equivalent statement is:

```
SELECT
CustomerName,
QuantityPurchased
FROM Purchases
WHERE QuantityPurchased BETWEEN 5 AND 20
```

In both cases, the SELECT returns this data:

CustomerName	QuantityPurchased
Carol White	10
James Carpenter	5

The BETWEEN operator always requires a corresponding AND placed between the two numbers.

Note the relative simplicity of the BETWEEN operator. Also notice that the BETWEEN is inclusive of the numbers specified. In this example, BETWEEN 5 AND 20 includes the numbers 5 and 20. Thus, the BETWEEN is equivalent only to the greater than or equal to (>=) and less than or equal to (<=) operators. It can't be used to express something simply greater than (>) or less than (<) a range of numbers. The row for James Carpenter is selected because the quantity purchased is equal to 5, and therefore is between 5 and 20.

The NOT operator can be used in conjunction with BETWEEN. For example, this SELECT:

```
SELECT
CustomerName,
QuantityPurchased
FROM Purchases
WHERE QuantityPurchased NOT BETWEEN 5 AND 20
```

retrieves this data:

CustomerName	QuantityPurchased
Andrew Li	4

The IN Operator

Just as BETWEEN represents a special case of the AND operator, the IN operator allows for a special case of the OR operator. Let's say we want to see rows where the state is Illinois or New York. Without the IN operator, this can be accomplished with this statement:

```
SELECT
CustomerName,
State
FROM Purchases
WHERE State = 'IL'
OR State = 'NY'
```

Here is an equivalent statement using the IN operator:

```
SELECT
CustomerName,
State
FROM Purchases
WHERE State IN ('IL', 'NY')
```

In either case, the data retrieved is:

CustomerName	State
Andrew Li	IL
James Carpenter	NY

The IN operator requires a subsequent listing of values enclosed within parentheses. Commas must be used to separate all values.

The usefulness of the IN operator may not be obvious in this example, where only two states are listed. However, the IN can just as easily be used in situations involving dozens of specific values. This greatly reduces the amount of typing required for such a statement. Another handy use for the IN operator comes in situations where values are obtained from an Excel spreadsheet. To obtain multiple values from adjacent cells in a spreadsheet for a SQL statement, you merely need to copy those values with a comma delimiter. The values can then be pasted inside parentheses following the IN operator.

As with the BETWEEN operator, the NOT operator can be used with the IN operator, as shown in this example:

```
SELECT
CustomerName,
State
FROM Purchases
WHERE State NOT IN ('IL', 'NY')
```

This retrieves this data:

CustomerName	State
Carol White	CA

One final note about the IN operator. There is a second way to use the IN operator that is substantially different from the syntax just discussed. In the second format, an entire SELECT statement is specified within parentheses, allowing the individual values to be created logically when needed. This is called a *subquery*, which will be covered in detail in Chapter 14.

Boolean Logic and NULL Values

At the beginning of this chapter, we stated that the Boolean logic in SQL evaluates complex expressions as either true or false. This assertion was not completely accurate. When evaluating the conditions in a WHERE clause, there are actually three possibilities: true, false, and unknown. The possibility of an unknown value derives from the fact that columns in SQL databases are sometimes allowed to have a NULL value. As mentioned in Chapter 1, NULL values are those for which there is an absence of data.

SQL provides a special keyword to test for the presence of NULL values for a column specified in a WHERE clause. The keyword is IS NULL. Let's look at an example taken from the Products table seen previously:

ProductID	Description	Weight
1	Printer A	NULL
2	Printer B	0
3	Monitor C	2
4	Laptop D	4

For this example, we'll imagine that as rows are added to the Products table, they are initially not given a weight. The Weight column is initially given a value of NULL, and a user later assigns a weight to the product.

Let's say that we attempt to use the following SELECT to find products missing a weight:

```
SELECT
Description,
Weight
FROM Products
WHERE Weight = 0
```

This would return:

Description	Weight
Printer B	0

This is not quite what we want. A weight of zero is not the same as a weight with a NULL value. To correct this, we need to issue:

```
SELECT
Description,
Weight
FROM Products
WHERE Weight = 0
OR Weight IS NULL
```

This returns:

Description	Weight
Printer A	NULL
Printer B	0

The IS NULL keyword can also be negated as IS NOT NULL, which allows for the retrieval of rows that do not have NULL for the specified column.

Note that the ISNULL function, discussed in Chapter 4, can provide an alternative to the IS NULL keyword. The equivalent of the previous SELECT statement, using the ISNULL function, is:

```
SELECT
Description,
Weight
FROM Products
WHERE ISNULL(Weight, 0) = 0
```

This SELECT retrieves the same two rows. The ISNULL function converts all values for the Weight column with a value of NULL to 0. This produces the same result as the previous statement, which tested for a value of 0 or NULL.

The ISNULL function and IS NULL keywords can also be used together, as in this statement:

```
SELECT
Description,
ISNULL(Weight, 0) AS 'Weight'
FROM Products
WHERE Weight = 0
OR Weight IS NULL
```

This produces this data:

Description	Weight
Printer A	0
Printer B	0

Looking Ahead

This chapter covered the important topic of how to create complex expressions of selection logic. The basic Boolean operators used in this endeavor were AND, OR, and NOT. We also discussed the BETWEEN and IN operators, which allow for a more concise statement of the AND and OR operators in certain situations. Parentheses are another essential tool in the formulation of complex expressions. By using parentheses, you can create almost every imaginable logical condition. Finally, we discussed how to deal with NULL values when selecting data.

In our next chapter, we'll revisit the *columnlist* and explore an important construct that will allow us to inject logic into the individual columns in the *columnlist*. This is referred to as *conditional logic*. By using the same Boolean logic operators discussed in this chapter, along with a few additional keywords, we'll be able to specify logic that determines how individual columns in the *columnlist* are displayed.

8

Conditional Logic

Keywords Introduced

CASE · WHEN · THEN · ELSE · END

The main topic of this chapter is *conditional logic*. This term refers to an ability to infuse logic into the values that appear in specific columns in a *columnlist* or other expressions in a SQL statement. Based on how the logic is evaluated when the SQL statement is executed, various values can appear for a column. Thus, values that appear are *conditional* on the specified logic. More specifically, conditional logic is indicated by an expression that begins with the CASE keyword. This is often referred to as a CASE expression. In essence, CASE expressions allow you to alter the output presented to a user, based on logical conditions, as applied to an evaluation of specific columns or data elements. The use of the word CASE has nothing to do with uppercase or lowercase. It's used in the sense of specifying a particular case, or a set of logic, in a conditional way.

As a beginning SQL developer, you should be aware that the CASE expression is a relatively advanced concept. You can get by without ever using CASE expressions and still write some very useful queries. Nevertheless, the ability to understand and use conditional logic can transform rudimentary queries into something a bit more sublime. As such, this is one of those topics that might merit an additional review after you've gone through the entire book, as a reminder of some of the interesting things can be accomplished with this technique.

The CASE Expression

The CASE expression in SQL allows logic to be applied to a single element in a *columnlist* or expression. As indicated in Chapter 2, the full format of the SELECT statement is:

```
SELECT columnlist
FROM tablelist
WHERE condition
GROUP BY columnlist
HAVING condition
ORDER BY columnlist
```

The CASE expression can appear in several areas of the SELECT statement. It can appear in the *columnlist* immediately after the SELECT keyword or in the GROUP BY or ORDER BY clauses. It can also appear as an element in a condition of the WHERE or HAVING clauses. In this chapter, we'll begin by illustrating the use of the CASE expression in a SELECT *columnlist*. This is its most typical use. We'll then follow up by also showing how it can be used in the WHERE and ORDER BY clauses.

The CASE expression replaces any individual column in a *columnlist* or an expression referenced in a condition in the WHERE or HAVING clause. Focusing on its use in a *columnlist*, a SELECT statement that includes both columns and a CASE expression might look like this:

```
SELECT
column1,
column2,
CaseExpression
FROM table
```

The CASE expression itself contains logic embedded in a traditional IF-THEN-ELSE structure. The term IF-THEN-ELSE refers to a commonly used logical construct employed by procedural programming languages. In general terms, this type of logic looks like:

```
IF some condition is true
THEN do this
ELSE do that
```

The condition expressed in the IF-THEN-ELSE can contain the full range of Boolean logic discussed in the previous chapter. Thus, the expression can include the AND, OR, NOT, BETWEEN, and IN operators, as well as parentheses.

The Simple CASE Format

There are two basic formats for the CASE expression, generally referred to as the *simple* and the *searched*. The simple format is:

```
CASE ColumnOrExpression
WHEN value1 THEN result1
WHEN value2 THEN result2
(repeat WHEN-THEN any number of times)
[ELSE DefaultResult]
END
```

As you can see, this CASE expression uses a number of keywords besides CASE; it also includes WHEN, THEN, ELSE, and END. These additional keywords are needed to fully define the logic of the CASE expression. The WHEN and THEN keywords define a condition that is evaluated. If the value after the WHEN is true, then the result after THEN is used. The WHEN and THEN keywords can be repeated any number of times. When there is a WHEN, there must also be a corresponding THEN. The ELSE keyword is used to define a default value to be used if none of the WHEN-THEN conditions is true. As indicated by the brackets, the ELSE keyword is not required. However, it is usually a good idea to include the ELSE keyword in every CASE expression to explicitly state a default value. The END keyword terminates the CASE expression.

Let's look at a specific example, using this Groceries table:

GroceryID	CategoryCode	Description
1	F	Apple
2	F	Orange
3	S	Mustard
4	V	Carrot
5	B	Water

In this data, the CategoryCode column is meant to have these meanings: F is fruit, S is spice, V is vegetable, and B is beverage. A SELECT with a CASE expression for data in this table might look like this:

```
SELECT
CASE CategoryCode
WHEN 'F' THEN 'Fruit'
WHEN 'V' THEN 'Vegetable'
ELSE 'Other'
END AS 'Category',
Description
FROM Groceries
```

and produces this output:

Category	Description
Fruit	Apple
Fruit	Orange
Other	Mustard
Vegetable	Carrot
Other	Water

Let's examine the SELECT statement in some detail. The first line contains the SELECT keyword. The second line, with the CASE keyword, specifies that the CategoryCode column is to be analyzed. The third line introduces the first WHEN-THEN condition. This line says that if the CategoryCode column equals F, then "Fruit" should be displayed. The next line says that if the CategoryCode is V, then "Vegetable" should be displayed. The ELSE line provides a default value of "Other" to use if the CategoryCode is not F or V. In other words, if the category is not Fruit or Vegetable, then it can be classified as "Other". The END line terminates the CASE expression and also includes an AS keyword to assign a column alias. The next line, Description, is merely another column and has nothing to do with the CASE expression.

As seen, the CASE expression is very useful for translating cryptic values into meaningful descriptions. In this example, the CategoryCode column in the Groceries table contains only a single character code to indicate the type of product. The CASE expression allows us to specify the translation.

The Searched CASE Format

The general format for the *searched* CASE expression is:

```
CASE
WHEN condition1 THEN result1
WHEN condition2 THEN result2
(repeat WHEN-THEN any number of times)
[ELSE DefaultResult]
END
```

The equivalent of the preceding SELECT statement using this second format is:

```
SELECT
CASE
WHEN CategoryCode = 'F' THEN 'Fruit'
WHEN CategoryCode = 'V' THEN 'Vegetable'
ELSE 'Other'
END AS 'Category',
Description
FROM Groceries
```

The data retrieved from this statement is identical to the first simple CASE format. Notice the subtle differences, however. In the simple format, the column name to be evaluated is placed after the CASE keyword, and the expression following the WHEN is a simple literal value. In the searched format, a column name to be evaluated is not placed next to the CASE keyword. Instead, this format allows for a more complex conditional expression to be specified following the WHEN keyword.

In the previous example, either format of the CASE clause can be used and will produce the same result. Let's now look at another example for which only the searched CASE format yields the desired result. This example will be taken from this data:

GroceryID	Fruit	Vegetable	Spice	Beverage	Description
1	X				Apple
2	X				Orange
3			X		Mustard
4		X			Carrot
5				X	Water

In this situation, rather than containing a single CategoryCode column, the table has multiple columns to indicate the type of product. For example, a value of X in the Fruit column is used to indicate that the product is a fruit. As such, it would be impossible to use the simple format of the CASE expression to evaluate this data. The simple format works only with an analysis of a single column. Using the searched format, a CASE expression that handles this type of data is:

```
SELECT
CASE
WHEN Fruit = 'X' THEN 'Fruit'
WHEN Vegetable = 'X' THEN 'Vegetable'
ELSE 'Other'
END AS 'Category',
Description
FROM GroceryCategories
```

Once again, the result is:

Category	Description
Fruit	Apple
Fruit	Orange
Other	Mustard
Vegetable	Carrot
Other	Water

We have been able to use the searched format of the CASE expression to evaluate data in multiple columns to produce a single result.

The CASE expression can be employed in many situations in the *columnlist* of a SELECT statement. Another common example of the usefulness of the CASE expression is in situations involving division by zero. When formulating a calculation that has the possibility of division by zero, you must be careful to provide some alternative when the denominator equals zero. Like all other computer languages, SQL produces an error when division by zero is attempted. To resolve this issue, a CASE expression can be used, as in this general example:

```
SELECT
CASE
WHEN Denominator = 0 THEN 0
ELSE Numerator / Denominator
END
FROM table
```

In this example, we're testing the denominator value to see if it equals zero. If it does, the result of the calculation is set to zero. If not, the normal calculation is allowed to proceed. Thus, if the denominator in the calculation happens to have a value of zero, we'll bypass the "divide by zero" error that would otherwise ensue.

Conditional Logic in ORDER BY Clauses

As mentioned at the beginning of this chapter, the CASE expression can be used in numerous places in the SELECT statement. To illustrate its use in the ORDER BY clause, let's imagine that we have a table with cities from the US and Canada. In this scenario, there are separate columns for US States and Canadian Provinces. This data might appear as the following:

CityID	Country	State	Province	City
1	US	VT		Burlington
2	CA		QU	Montreal
3	US	CO		Denver
4	US	CO		Boulder
5	CA		AB	Edmonton

The goal in this example is to sort data first by country, and then by either state or province, and finally by city. A statement that accomplishes this is:

```
SELECT *
FROM NorthAmerica
ORDER BY
Country,
CASE Country
WHEN 'US' THEN State
WHEN 'CA' THEN Province
ELSE State
END,
City
```

The output from this statement is:

CityID	Country	State	Province	City
5	CA		AB	Edmonton
2	CA		QU	Montreal
4	US	CO		Boulder
3	US	CO		Denver
1	US	VT		Burlington

The CASE expression evaluates the Country column to determine whether it's US or CA. If it's US data, then it uses the State column for the sort. If Canada, it uses Province. The result is that this statement sorts by country, then by state or province, and finally by city.

Conditional Logic in WHERE Clauses

Just as the CASE expression can be placed within a *columnlist*, it can also be placed within an expression in a WHERE condition. In this example, we'll assume that we have customer data such as the following:

CustomerID	Sex	Age	Income
1	M	55	80000
2	F	25	65000
3	M	35	40000
4	F	42	90000
5	F	27	25000

The goal is to select customers who meet a complex set of demographic and income requirements. If they are male and at least 50 years old, they must have an income of 75000 to qualify. If they are female and at least 35, they must have an income of 60000 to qualify. All other people must have income of at least 50000 to qualify. The following is a statement that specifies that criteria by using a CASE statement:

```
SELECT *
FROM CustomerList
WHERE Income >
CASE
WHEN Sex = 'M' AND Age >= 50 THEN 75000
WHEN Sex = 'F' AND Age >= 35 THEN 60000
ELSE 50000
END
```

Note that the entire CASE expression replaced just one part of the condition expressed in the WHERE clause. In general form, the WHERE clause is:

```
WHERE Income > CASE_Expression
```

The CASE expression provides the value that is compared to Income in the selection logic. When this statement is executed, the data retrieved is:

CustomerID	Sex	Age	Income
1	M	55	80000
2	F	25	65000
4	F	42	90000

Looking Ahead

The CASE expression is a powerful tool that allows you to infuse logic into various elements in a SQL statement. In this chapter, we saw the CASE expression used in the SELECT *columnlist*, and also in the ORDER BY and WHERE clauses. In future chapters, we'll illustrate the use of the CASE expression in other areas, such as in the GROUP BY and HAVING clauses.

There are two basic variations of the CASE expression: the *simple* and the *searched*. A typical use of the simple variation is to provide translations for data items with cryptic values. The searched format allows for more complex statements of logic.

In our next chapter, "Summarizing Data," we'll turn our attention to methods of separating data into groups and summarizing the values in those groups with various statistics. Back in Chapter 4, "Using Functions," we talked about scalar functions. The next chapter will introduce another type of function, called *aggregate functions*. These aggregate functions allow us to summarize data in many useful ways. For example, we'll be able to look at any group of orders and determine the number of orders, the total dollar amount of the orders, and the average order size. These techniques will allow you to move beyond the presentation of detailed data and begin to truly add value for your users as you deliver summarized information.

9

Summarizing Data

Keywords Introduced

DISTINCT · SUM · AVG · MIN · MAX · COUNT · GROUP BY · HAVING · ROW_NUMBER · RANK · DENSE RANK · NTILE · OVER · PARTITION BY

Up until now, all of the calculations, functions, and CASE expressions we've used have only altered the values of individual columns. The rows we've retrieved have corresponded to rows in tables in the underlying database. We now want to turn to various methods of summarizing data, by combining values in multiple rows.

The computer term usually associated with this type of endeavor is *aggregation*, which means "to combine into groups." The ability to aggregate and summarize data is key to being able to move beyond a mere display of data to something approaching real information. There's a bit of magic involved when users view summarized data in a report. The ability to summarize offers the opportunity of extracting some real meaning from the mass of data in a database in order to obtain a clearer picture of what it all means.

Eliminating Duplicates

Although it doesn't provide true aggregation, the most elementary way to summarize data is to eliminate duplicates. SQL's DISTINCT keyword provides an easy method for removing duplicate values from output. Here's an example of the DISTINCT keyword, used with the following SongTitles table:

SongID	Artist	Album	Title
1	The Beatles	Revolver	Yellow Submarine
2	The Beatles	Revolver	Eleanor Rigby
3	The Beatles	Abbey Road	Here Comes the Sun
4	The Rolling Stones	Beggars Banquet	Sympathy for the Devil
5	The Rolling Stones	Let It Bleed	Gimme Shelter
6	Paul McCartney	Ram	Too Many People

Let's say we want to see a list of artists in the table. This can be accomplished with:

```
SELECT
DISTINCT
Artist
FROM SongTitles
ORDER BY Artist
```

The result is:

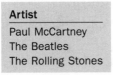

Artist
Paul McCartney
The Beatles
The Rolling Stones

The DISTINCT keyword is always placed immediately after the SELECT keyword. The DISTINCT keyword specifies that only unique values of the *columnlist* that follow are to be returned. In this case, there are only three artists, so only three rows are returned. If we want to see unique combinations of both artists and albums, we can issue:

```
SELECT
DISTINCT
Artist,
Album
FROM SongTitles
ORDER BY Artist, Album
```

and the result would be:

Artist	Album
Paul McCartney	Ram
The Beatles	Abbey Road
The Beatles	Revolver
The Rolling Stones	Beggars Banquet
The Rolling Stones	Let It Bleed

Notice that Revolver is listed only once, even though there are two songs from that album in the table. This is because the DISTINCT keyword only considers values from the listed columns.

Aggregate Functions

The functions discussed in Chapter 4, "Using Functions," were all *scalar functions*. These functions were all performed on a single number or value. In contrast, *aggregate functions* are meant to be used with groups of data. The most widely used aggregate functions are COUNT, SUM, AVG, MIN, and MAX. These functions provide counts, sums, averages, and minimum and maximum values for groups of data.

All of our aggregate function examples will be taken from the following two tables with data about student fees and grades. The Fees table contains:

FeeID	Student	FeeType	Fee
1	Jose	Gym	30
2	Jose	Lunch	10
3	Jose	Trip	8
4	Rama	Gym	30
5	Julie	Lunch	10

This is the Grades table:

GradeID	Student	GradeType	Grade	YearInSchool
1	Isabella	Quiz	92	7
2	Isabella	Quiz	95	7
3	Isabella	Homework	84	7
4	Hailey	Quiz	62	8
5	Hailey	Quiz	81	8
6	Hailey	Homework	NULL	8
7	Peter	Quiz	58	7
8	Peter	Quiz	74	7
9	Peter	Homework	88	7

Beginning with the SUM function, let's say we want to see the total amount of gym fees paid by all students. This can be accomplished with this statement:

```
SELECT
SUM(Fee) AS 'Total Gym Fees'
FROM Fees
WHERE FeeType = 'Gym'
```

The resulting data is:

Total Gym Fees
60

As you can see, the SUM function sums up the total values for the Fee column, subject to the selection logic specified in the WHERE clause. Because the only expression in the *columnlist* is an aggregate function, the query returns only one column and one row of data with the aggregate amount.

The AVG, MIN, and MAX functions are quite similar to the SUM function. Here's an example of the AVG function. In this case, we're seeking to obtain the average grade of all quizzes in the Grades table:

```
SELECT
AVG(Grade) AS 'Average Quiz Score'
FROM Grades
WHERE GradeType = 'Quiz'
```

The result is:

Average Quiz Score
77

More than one aggregate function can be used in a single statement. Here's a SELECT that shows how to utilize AVG, MIN, and MAX in the same statement:

```
SELECT
AVG(Grade) AS 'Average Quiz Score',
MIN(Grade) AS 'Minimum Quiz Score',
MAX(Grade) AS 'Maximum Quiz Score'
FROM Grades
WHERE GradeType = 'Quiz'
```

The result is:

Average Quiz Score	Minimum Quiz Score	Maximum Quiz Score
77	58	95

The COUNT Function

The COUNT function is slightly more complex than the aggregate functions discussed previously, in that it can be employed in three different ways. First, the COUNT function can be used to return a count of all selected rows, regardless of the values in any particular column. As an example, the following statement returns a count of all rows that have homework grades:

```
SELECT
COUNT(*) AS 'Count of Homework Rows'
FROM Grades
WHERE GradeType = 'Homework'
```

The result is:

Count of Homework Rows
3

The asterisk within parentheses means "all columns." Behind the scenes, SQL actually retrieves the data in all columns for the selected rows, and then returns a count of the number of rows.

In the second format of the COUNT function, a specific column is specified within the parentheses. Here's an example:

```
SELECT
COUNT(Grade) AS 'Count of Homework Scores'
FROM Grades
WHERE GradeType = 'Homework'
```

The result is:

Count of Homework Rows
2

Notice the subtle difference between the preceding two SELECT statements. In the first, we're merely counting rows where the GradeType equals Homework. There are three of those rows. In the second statement, we're counting occurrences of the Grade column where the GradeType column has a value of Homework. In this case, one of the three rows has a value of NULL in the Grade column, and SQL is smart enough not to count such a row. As mentioned previously, NULL means that the data doesn't exist.

The third variant of the COUNT function allows us to use the DISTINCT keyword in addition to a column name. Here's an example:

```
SELECT
COUNT(DISTINCT FeeType) AS 'Number of Fee Types'
FROM Fees
```

Note that the DISTINCT keyword is placed inside the parentheses. The DISTINCT keyword says that we want to include only distinct values of FeeType. The outer COUNT function counts those values. The result of this statement is:

Number of Fee Types
3

This means that there are three different values found in the FeeType column.

Grouping Data

The previous examples of aggregation functions are interesting but of somewhat limited value. The real power of aggregation functions will become evident after we introduce the concept of grouping data.

The GROUP BY keyword is used to separate the data returned from a SELECT statement into any number of groups. For example, when looking at the Grades table, we may be interested in analyzing test scores based on the grade type. In other words, we want to separate the data into two separate groups: quizzes and homework. The value of the GradeType column can be used to determine the group to which each row belongs. Once data has been separated into groups, aggregation functions can be used so that summary statistics for each of the groups can be calculated and compared.

Let's proceed with an example that introduces the GROUP BY keyword:

```
SELECT
GradeType AS 'Grade Type',
AVG(Grade) AS 'Average Grade'
FROM Grades
GROUP BY GradeType
ORDER BY GradeType
```

The result of this statement is:

Grade Type	Average Grade
Homework	86
Quiz	77

In this example, the GROUP BY keyword specifies that groups are to be created based on the value of the GradeType column. The two columns in the SELECT *columnlist* are GradeType and a calculated field that uses the AVG function. The GradeType column was included in the *columnlist* because, when creating a group, it's usually a good idea to include the column on which the groups are based. The "Average Grade" calculated field aggregates values based on the rows in each group.

Notice that the average homework grade has been computed as 86. As before, even though there is one row with a NULL value for the Homework GradeType, SQL is smart enough to ignore rows with NULL values when computing an average. If we had wanted the NULL value to be counted as a 0, then the ISNULL function could be used to convert the NULL to a 0, as follows:

```
AVG(ISNULL(Grade, 0)) AS 'Average Grade'
```

It's important to note that when using a GROUP BY keyword, all columns in the *columnlist* must either be listed as columns in the GROUP BY clause, or else be used in an aggregation function. Nothing else would make any sense. For example, the following SELECT would produce a syntax error:

```
SELECT
GradeType AS 'Grade Type',
AVG(Grade) AS 'Average Grade',
Student AS 'Student'
FROM Grades
GROUP BY GradeType
ORDER BY GradeType
```

The problem with this statement is that the Student column is not in the GROUP BY, nor is it aggregated in any way. Since everything is presented in summarized groups, SQL doesn't know what to do with the Student column in the above statement. As such, this statement cannot be executed.

Database Differences: MySQL

Unlike Microsoft SQL Server and Oracle, the previous statement will not produce an error in MySQL. Nevertheless, it will produce incorrect results.

Multiple Columns and Sorting

The concept of groups can be extended so that groups are based on more than one column. Let's go back to the last SELECT and add the Student column to both the GROUP BY clause and the *columnlist*. It now looks like:

```
SELECT
GradeType AS 'Grade Type',
Student AS 'Student',
AVG(Grade) AS 'Average Grade'
FROM Grades
GROUP BY GradeType, Student
ORDER BY GradeType, Student
```

The resulting data is:

Grade Type	Student	Average Grade
Homework	Hailey	NULL
Homework	Isabella	84
Homework	Peter	88
Quiz	Hailey	71.5
Quiz	Isabella	93.5
Quiz	Peter	66

We now see a breakdown not only of grade types but also of students. The average grades are computed on each group. Note that the Homework row for Hailey shows a NULL value, since she has only one homework row, and that row has a value of NULL for the grade.

The order in which the columns are listed in the GROUP BY clause has no significance. The results would be the same if the clause were:

```
GROUP BY Student, GradeType
```

However, as always, the order in which columns are listed in the ORDER BY clause is meaningful. If you switch the ORDER BY clause to:

```
ORDER BY Student, GradeType
```

The resulting data is:

GradeType	Student	AverageGrade
Homework	Hailey	NULL
Quiz	Hailey	71.5
Homework	Isabella	84
Quiz	Isabella	93.5
Homework	Peter	88
Quiz	Peter	66

This looks a bit strange, because it's difficult to determine at a glance that the data is really sorted by Student and then by GradeType. As a general rule of thumb, it usually helps if columns are listed from left to right in the same order in which columns are sorted. A more understandable SELECT statement would be:

```
SELECT
Student AS 'Student',
GradeType AS 'Grade Type',
AVG(Grade) AS 'Average Grade'
FROM Grades
GROUP BY GradeType, Student
ORDER BY Student, GradeType
```

The data now looks like this:

Student	Grade Type	Average Grade
Hailey	Homework	NULL
Hailey	Quiz	71.5
Isabella	Homework	84
Isabella	Quiz	93.5
Peter	Homework	88
Peter	Quiz	66

This is more comprehensible, because the column order corresponds to the sort order.

There's sometimes some confusion as to the difference between the GROUP BY and ORDER BY clauses. The main point to remember is that GROUP BY merely creates the groups. The ORDER BY still must be used to list the rows in a meaningful sequence.

Selection Criteria on Aggregates

After data has been separated into groups via the GROUP BY clause, selection criteria become a bit more complex. When applying any kind of selection criteria to a SELECT with a GROUP BY, you must ask whether the criteria apply to individual rows or to the entire group. Whereas the WHERE clause handles selection criteria for individual rows, SQL provides a keyword named HAVING that allows selection logic to be applied at the group level.

Returning to the Grades table, let's say we want to look only at grades on quizzes that are 70 or higher. The grades we'd like to look at are individual grades, so the WHERE clause can be used, as normal. Such a SELECT might look like this:

```
SELECT
Student AS 'Student',
GradeType AS 'Grade Type',
Grade AS 'Grade'
FROM Grades
WHERE GradeType = 'Quiz'
AND Grade >= 70
ORDER BY Student, Grade
```

The resulting data is:

Student	Grade Type	Grade
Hailey	Quiz	81
Isabella	Quiz	92
Isabella	Quiz	95
Peter	Quiz	74

Notice that quizzes with a score less than 70 aren't shown. For example, we can see Peter's quiz score of 74, but not his quiz score of 58.

To introduce the use of the HAVING clause, let's say we want to display data for students who have an *average* quiz grade of 70 or more. In this situation, we want to select on an average, not on individual rows. This is where the HAVING clause comes in. We need to first group grades by student, and then apply selection criteria to an aggregate statistic based on the entire group. The following statement produces the desired result:

```
SELECT
Student AS 'Student',
AVG(Grade) AS 'Average Quiz Grade'
FROM Grades
WHERE GradeType = 'Quiz'
GROUP BY Student
HAVING AVG(Grade) >= 70
ORDER BY Student
```

The output is:

Student	Average Quiz Grade
Hailey	71.5
Isabella	93.5

This SELECT has both a WHERE and a HAVING clause. The WHERE ensures that we only select rows with a GradeType of "Quiz". The HAVING guarantees that we only select students with an average score of at least 70.

To take this example a step further, what if we wanted to add a column with the GradeType value? If we attempt to add GradeType to the SELECT *columnlist*, the statement will error. This is because all columns must be either listed in the GROUP BY or involved in an aggregation. Hence, if we want to show the GradeType column, it must be added to the GROUP BY clause, as follows:

```
SELECT
Student AS 'Student',
GradeType AS 'Grade Type',
AVG(Grade) AS 'Average Grade'
FROM Grades
WHERE GradeType = 'Quiz'
GROUP BY Student, GradeType
HAVING AVG(Grade) >= 70
ORDER BY Student
```

The resulting data is:

Student	Grade Type	Average Grade
Hailey	Quiz	71.5
Isabella	Quiz	93.5

Now that we've added the HAVING clause to the mix, let's recap the general format of the SELECT statement with all the clauses used thus far:

```
SELECT columnlist
FROM tablelist
WHERE condition
GROUP BY columnlist
HAVING condition
ORDER BY columnlist
```

Remember that when employing any of the above keywords in a SELECT, they must be listed in the order shown. For example, the HAVING keyword must always come after a GROUP BY but before an ORDER BY.

Conditional Logic in GROUP BY Clauses

In Chapter 8, "Conditional Logic," we saw examples of the CASE expression in the *columnlist* of a SELECT statement as well as in the ORDER BY and WHERE clauses. When a GROUP BY clause is used in a statement, all expressions in the *columnlist* must either be present in the GROUP BY or involve an aggregate function. This means that when a CASE expression is used in a GROUP BY, the same exact expression must be used in the SELECT *columnlist*. To illustrate, let's return to the Groceries data seen in the previous chapter:

GroceryID	CategoryCode	Description
1	F	Apple
2	F	Orange
3	S	Mustard
4	V	Carrot
5	B	Water

In this example, we want to group by the category computed by the CASE expression—namely, Fruit, Vegetable, or Other. The objective is to produce a count of how many products are in each category. Here's the statement:

```
SELECT
CASE CategoryCode
WHEN 'F' THEN 'Fruit'
WHEN 'V' THEN 'Vegetable'
ELSE 'Other'
END AS 'Category',
COUNT(*) AS 'Count'
FROM Groceries
GROUP BY
CASE CategoryCode
WHEN 'F' THEN 'Fruit'
WHEN 'V' THEN 'Vegetable'
ELSE 'Other'
END
```

The output appears as:

Category	Count
Fruit	2
Other	2
Vegetable	1

Notice that the same CASE statement is used in the SELECT *columnlist* and in the GROUP BY clause.

Conditional Logic in HAVING Clauses

To illustrate the use of conditional logic in HAVING clauses, let's return to the HAVING clause example from earlier in this chapter. In that situation, we displayed data for students who had an average quiz grade of 70 or higher. The statement was:

```
SELECT
Student AS 'Student',
GradeType AS 'Grade Type',
AVG(Grade) AS 'Average Grade'
FROM Grades
WHERE GradeType = 'Quiz'
GROUP BY Student, GradeType
HAVING AVG(Grade) >= 70
ORDER BY Student
```

In this scenario, the WHERE clause selected quizzes. We declared a GROUP BY student and grade type and then applied the aggregate selection logic in the HAVING clause to enforce the restriction that we want only students with an average quiz of at least 70.

In this new example, we'll use a column in the data that was previously ignored—namely, the YearInSchool column. With this additional bit of information, we'll alter the previous statement to list students with an average grade of at least 70 if they're a Year 7 student, or an average grade of 75 if they're a Year 8 student. If they're not Year 7 or Year 8, we'll accept students with an average grade of 80. To accomplish this goal, we'll need to place a CASE expression in the HAVING clause. We'll also display the YearInSchool column, as follows:

```
SELECT
Student AS 'Student',
YearInSchool AS 'Year in School',
GradeType AS 'Grade Type',
AVG(Grade) AS 'Average Grade',
FROM Grades
WHERE GradeType = 'Quiz'
GROUP BY Student, YearInSchool, GradeType
HAVING AVG(Grade) >=
CASE
WHEN YearInSchool = 7 THEN 70
WHEN YearInSchool = 8 THEN 75
ELSE 80
END
ORDER BY Student
```

The HAVING clause states that the average grade must be greater than the number returned by the CASE expression. The CASE expression will provide a value of either 70, 75, or 80, depending on the value of the YearInSchool column. The result is:

Student	Year in School	Grade Type	Average Grade
Isabella	7	Quiz	93.5

Isabella is now the only student listed, because she is only person who satisfies the new criteria.

Ranking Functions

In addition to the grouping techniques discussed previously in this chapter, SQL provides a number of special *ranking* functions that allow for the classification of rows by a method of sequential classification. There are four basic ranking functions:

```
Row_Number
Rank
Dense_Rank
NTile
```

The ROW_NUMBER function creates row numbers based on a specified order of another column or expression associated with the function. After the rows have been placed in the specified order, the generated row numbers will start with 1 and increase sequentially to 2, 3, 4, and so on. The ROW_NUMBER function requires no parameters.

The RANK function is the same as ROW_NUMBER except that if two or more rows have the same value for the specified column or expression, they are both given the same number. For example, if the second and third rows have the same value, the generated ranks will be 1, 2, 2, 4, and so on. Because the two rows with a value of 2 have the same value, SQL skips the number 3.

The DENSE_RANK function is the same as the RANK function except that it does not skip any numbers, even when there are duplicate values. In the preceding example, the dense rank would be 1, 2, 2, 3, and so on. The number 3 is not skipped.

Finally, the NTILE function allows for the generation of a percentile or any other ntile, based on the specified order of another column or expression. Unlike RANK, ROW_NUMBER, and DENSE_RANK, NTILE requires a parameter. For example, the function NTILE(100) will assign percentiles. Percentiles are a number from 1 to 100 that represents the relative rank of the value. However, any other number can be used as the argument for the function. Thus, the function NTILE(10) will create deciles, and NTILE(4) will produce quartiles.

Let's illustrate ranking with a few examples, all based on the following table:

StockSymbol	StockName	Exchange	PriceEarningsRatio
AAPL	Apple Inc	NASDAQ	14
AMZN	Amazon.com Inc	NASDAQ	489
DIS	The Walt Disney Company	NYSE	21
GE	General Electric Company	NYSE	18
GOOG	Alphabet Inc	NASDAQ	30
HSY	The Hershey Company	NYSE	26
KRFT	Kraft Foods Inc	NYSE	12
KO	The Coca-Cola Company	NYSE	21
MCD	McDonalds Corporation	NYSE	18
MMM	3M Company	NYSE	20
MSFT	Microsoft Corporation	NASDAQ	15
ORCL	Oracle Corporation	NASDAQ	17
SBUX	Starbucks Corporation	NASDAQ	357
WBA	Walgreens Boots Alliance Inc	NYSE	24
WMT	Wal-Mart Stores Inc	NYSE	15

This table lists some stocks, showing their symbol, their name, the exchange they trade on, and their price–earnings (PE) ratio. For example, Apple (AAPL) is traded on the NASDAQ and has a PE ratio of 14.

In this first example, we'll sort all the rows by PE ratio and use the ROW_NUMBER function to generate a row number for each row. We want to sort the rows by PE from lowest to highest. We're displaying low PE's first, since a low PE is generally better than a high PE. A statement that accomplishes this is:

```
SELECT
ROW_NUMBER() OVER (ORDER BY PriceEarningsRatio) AS 'Row',
StockSymbol AS 'Symbol',
StockName AS 'Name',
Exchange AS 'Exchange',
PriceEarningsRatio AS 'PE Ratio'
FROM Stocks
ORDER BY PriceEarningsRatio
```

The output of this statement is:

Row	Symbol	Name	Exchange	PE Ratio
1	KRFT	Kraft Foods Inc	NYSE	12
2	AAPL	Apple Inc	NASDAQ	14
3	MSFT	Microsoft Corporation	NASDAQ	15
4	WMT	Wal-Mart Stores Inc	NYSE	15
5	ORCL	Oracle Corporation	NASDAQ	17
6	GE	General Electric Company	NYSE	18
7	MCD	McDonald's Corporation	NYSE	18
8	MMM	3M Company	NYSE	20
9	DIS	The Walt Disney Company	NYSE	21
10	KO	The Coca-Cola Company	NYSE	21
11	WBA	Walgreens Boots Alliance Inc	NYSE	24
12	HSY	The Hershey Company	NYSE	26
13	GOOG	Alphabet Inc	NASDAQ	30
14	SBUX	Starbucks Corporation	NASDAQ	357
15	AMZN	Amazon.com Inc	NASDAQ	489

Let's examine how this works. First, note that there are no selection criteria or grouping in this statement. Besides the *columnlist*, there is only a FROM clause and an ORDER BY clause. The ORDER BY clause (the last line of the statement) is necessary to list the rows in the desired order, by PE ratio. The main bit of complexity in this statement is the first item in the *columnlist*, which uses the ROW_NUMBER ranking function. Note that this value includes an OVER keyword as well as another ORDER BY in parentheses. The general format for a *columnlist* element that includes a ranking function is:

```
Rank_Function() OVER (ORDER BY expression [[ASC]|DESC])
```

The *Rank_Function* can be any of the four functions mentioned previously. The keyword OVER is required. Its purpose is to designate how the rank function is to be applied. The *expression* in the parentheses indicates the column or expression on which the ranking is to be applied. The ORDER BY keyword indicates that this expression is to evaluated, in either an ascending or descending order. If the order is to be ascending, then the ASC keyword isn't necessary.

In our example, we're assigning a row number based on an evaluation of the PriceEarningsRatio column. The values of PriceEarningsRatio are evaluated in an ascending order. The first row, for Kraft Foods, is given a row number of 1 because it is first in the sequence. Note that the ROW_NUMBER function only assigns the row number. We still need the ORDER BY clause in the SELECT statement to actually display the output in the desired sequence.

To illustrate the use of the RANK and DENSE_RANK functions, we'll add them as columns to the previous statement. We won't bother to display the stock name or exchange. The new statement is:

```
SELECT
ROW_NUMBER() OVER (ORDER BY PriceEarningsRatio) AS 'Row',
RANK() OVER (ORDER BY PriceEarningsRatio) AS 'Rank',
DENSE_RANK() OVER (ORDER BY PriceEarningsRatio) AS 'Dense Rank',
StockSymbol AS 'Symbol',
PriceEarningsRatio AS 'PE Ratio'
FROM Stocks
ORDER BY PriceEarningsRatio
```

The output is:

Row	Rank	Dense Rank	Symbol	PE Ratio
1	1	1	KRFT	12
2	2	2	AAPL	14
3	3	3	MSFT	15
4	3	3	WMT	15
5	5	4	ORCL	17
6	6	5	GE	18
7	6	5	MCD	18
8	8	6	MMM	20
9	9	7	DIS	21
10	9	7	KO	21
11	11	8	WBA	24
12	12	9	HSY	26
13	13	10	GOOG	30
14	14	11	SBUX	357
15	15	12	AMZN	489

In this example, MSFT and WMT have the same PE. As a result, they are given the same value for RANK and for DENSE_RANK. The difference is in the values assigned to subsequent rows. For RANK, the next row after MSFT and WMT, ORCL, skips a number and is given a value of 5. For DENSE_RANK, no numbers are skipped, and ORCL is given a value of 4.

Moving on to the NTILE function, we'll offer examples of NTILE(4) and NTILE(10). As mentioned, the NTILE ranks the rows in a specified sequence, and then assigns them to a group. In the case of NTILE(4), the data is divided into four groups. This is commonly referred to as *quartiles*. NTILE(10) divides the data into ten groups, otherwise known as *deciles*. To illustrate, the following statement ranks the stocks by PE ratio and displays NTILE(4) and NTILE(10):

```
SELECT
NTILE(4) OVER (ORDER BY PriceEarningsRatio) AS 'Quartile',
NTILE(10) OVER (ORDER BY PriceEarningsRatio) AS 'Decile',
StockSymbol AS 'Symbol',
PriceEarningsRatio AS 'PE Ratio'
FROM Stocks
ORDER BY PriceEarningsRatio
```

The resulting output is:

Quartile	Decile	Symbol	PE Ratio
1	1	KRFT	12
1	1	AAPL	14
1	2	MSFT	15
1	2	WMT	15
2	3	ORCL	17
2	3	GE	18
2	4	MCD	18
2	4	MMM	20
3	5	DIS	21
3	5	KO	21
3	6	WBA	24
3	7	HSY	26
4	8	GOOG	30
4	9	SBUX	357
4	10	AMZN	489

The Quartile column divides the data into four groups, based on a ranking of the PE ratio. As seen, rows 1 to 4 fall in the top quartile, rows 5 to 8 in the second quartile, and so on. The Decile column divides the data into ten groups in a similar manner. With larger data sets, it would be common to include an NTILE(100) function to divide the data into 100 groups. Each of these 100 groups is commonly referred to as a *percentile*.

Database Differences: MySQL

Unlike Microsoft SQL Server and Oracle, MySQL doesn't provide the OVER keyword or the ranking functions discussed in this section. Likewise, it doesn't provide the PARTITION BY keyword discussed in the following section.

Partitions

A useful variation on how the ranking functions discussed in the previous section can be used is the ability to divide data into *partitions* prior to the application of the ranking function. We indicated previously that the general format for a *columnlist* element that includes a ranking function is:

```
Rank_Function() OVER (ORDER BY expression [[ASC]|DESC])
```

The partitioning of data involves the PARTITION BY keyword. With partitioning, the general format for a *columnlist* element that includes a ranking function is:

```
Rank_Function() OVER (PARTITION BY expression_1
ORDER BY expression_2 [[ASC]|DESC])
```

In the previous examples, we had ignored the value of the Exchange column. With partitioning, we have the ability to separate, or *partition*, our data into two separate groups, based on the value of the Exchange column, which is either NYSE or NASDAQ. After the data is separated, the ranking functions are applied as seen previously.

To illustrate, let's revise the first query of the previous section that used the ROW_NUMBER function to rank the data, assigning a row number to each row based on the PE ratio. The original SQL statement was:

```
SELECT
ROW_NUMBER() OVER (ORDER BY PriceEarningsRatio) AS 'Row',
StockSymbol AS 'Symbol',
StockName AS 'Name',
Exchange AS 'Exchange',
PriceEarningsRatio AS 'PE Ratio'
FROM Stocks
ORDER BY PriceEarningsRatio
```

In our revision, we'll add the PARTITION BY keyword to the *columnlist* element with the ROW_NUMBER function. We'll also rearrange the order of the columns and the ORDER BY clause so that the data appears in a more comprehensible layout. The new statement is:

```
SELECT
Exchange AS 'Exchange',
ROW_NUMBER() OVER (PARTITION BY Exchange ORDER BY PriceEarningsRatio)
AS 'Exchange Rank',
StockSymbol AS 'Symbol',
PriceEarningsRatio AS 'PE Ratio'
FROM Stocks
ORDER BY Exchange, PriceEarningsRatio
```

The result is:

Exchange	Exchange Rank	Symbol	PE Ratio
NASDAQ	1	AAPL	14
NASDAQ	2	MSFT	15
NASDAQ	3	ORCL	17
NASDAQ	4	GOOG	30
NASDAQ	5	SBUX	357
NASDAQ	6	AMZN	489
NYSE	1	KRFT	12
NYSE	2	WMT	15
NYSE	3	GE	18
NYSE	4	MCD	18
NYSE	5	MMM	20
NYSE	6	DIS	21
NYSE	7	KO	21
NYSE	8	WBA	24
NYSE	9	HSY	26

Notice that we also changed the column alias for the ROW_NUMBER function from "Row" to "Exchange Rank". This was done because we now have two sets of data. It wouldn't make sense to refer to this column as a row number, because we have two sequential sets of numbers. Note that the ORDER BY clause must correspond to the PARTITION BY and RANKING BY expressions in the ranking function. If the data is partitioned and ranked in one way and sorted in another way, the results might be difficult to comprehend.

Remember that partitions are not the same as the GROUP BY clause seen earlier in this chapter. The usual purpose of a GROUP BY clause is to group data and then to apply aggregation functions to each of the groups. For example, one might wish to group by the Exchange column and then obtain the average PE for each of the groups. This would provide the average PE for both the NASDAQ and NYSE exchanges. In contrast, the concept of partitioning keeps the detailed data intact. Partitions are created merely to apply a ranking to individual rows within each partition. Although data is divided into groups for purposes of ranking, the details are maintained, and there is no aggregation involved.

The preceding example illustrated the use of partitions with the ROW_NUMBER ranking function. The application of partitions to the other three ranking functions works in an identical manner. For example, if we wanted to partition the data based on the Exchange, and then show the quartile for each partition, the statement would be:

```
SELECT
Exchange AS 'Exchange',
NTILE(4) OVER (PARTITION BY Exchange ORDER BY PriceEarningsRatio)
AS 'Quartile',
StockSymbol AS 'Symbol',
PriceEarningsRatio AS 'PE Ratio'
FROM Stocks
ORDER BY Exchange, PriceEarningsRatio
```

The output for this statement is:

Exchange	Quartile	Symbol	PE Ratio
NASDAQ	1	AAPL	14
NASDAQ	1	MSFT	15
NASDAQ	2	ORCL	17
NASDAQ	2	GOOG	30
NASDAQ	3	SBUX	357
NASDAQ	4	AMZN	489
NYSE	1	KRFT	12
NYSE	1	WMT	15
NYSE	1	GE	18
NYSE	2	MCD	18
NYSE	2	MMM	20
NYSE	3	DIS	21
NYSE	3	KO	21
NYSE	4	WBA	24
NYSE	4	HSY	26

As expected, the data now shows a ranking of rows by quartile, for both NASDAQ and NYSE stocks.

The examples of ranking functions and partitions given thus far are interesting, but a much more useful application of these techniques will be seen in Chapter 14, "Subqueries." The ability to divide data into partitions and then apply a ranking to each partition means that we can specify a *top n* type of selection for each partition in a data set. For example, say that we want to select the largest order for each customer. We can partition the data by customer number, and then rank each row by the order amount. Ultimately, we want to select only one order per customer. This can be done by including a line such as the following in the query:

```
ROW_NUMBER() OVER
(PARTITION BY CustomerNumber ORDER BY OrderAmount) AS TheRow
```

This would have the effect of creating a calculated field named TheRow that ranks the orders for each customer by OrderAmount. The order with the highest value would be assigned a value of 1. As you'll see in Chapter 14, it is then possible to select from the results of the initial query, selecting only those rows where TheRow equals 1. This would give us the largest order for each customer. This technique can be applied in many similar situations. For example, we might want to see the most recent order for each customer or perhaps the most profitable customer in each city.

Looking Ahead

In this chapter, we covered several forms of aggregation, beginning with the simplest—that of eliminating duplicates. We then introduced a number of aggregate functions, which are a different class of functions from the scalar functions seen in Chapter 4. The real power of aggregate functions becomes apparent when they are used in conjunction with the GROUP BY keyword, which allows for the separation of data into groups. We also looked at the use of the HAVING clause, which allows you to apply group-level selection criteria to values in aggregate functions.

We closed this chapter with two additional topics related to summation. The use of CASE expressions in the GROUP BY and HAVING clauses allows you to apply conditional logic grouping and group selection criteria. Finally, we covered ranking functions and partitioning, which are useful ways of organizing detailed data. Through the use of the PARTITION BY keyword, data can be separated into groups in conjunction with the ranking functions.

Our next chapter, on subtotals and crosstabs, offers additional formatting options for aggregated values. Subtotals allow you to add summarized information to a presentation of detailed data. Crosstabs offer a new method of laying out data in a format that is more conducive to a clear display of aggregated data.

10

Subtotals and Crosstabs

Keywords Introduced

ROLLUP · GROUPING · CUBE · PIVOT · FOR

The previous chapter provided numerous ways to add aggregation to a query. We now want to extend that discussion to cover the additional option of providing subtotals. When we aggregate data, we're also removing the detailed data that lies below the summarized totals. The whole point of aggregation is to replace detailed data with a summarization. However, users sometimes want to see the detailed data, along with an occasional summary. This is where subtotals come in. Subtotals are typically provided via extra rows added in with the detailed data that summarize key columns.

A second topic we'll cover in this chapter has to do with how summarized data is displayed to the user. In the previous chapter, data was grouped together and then displayed to the user. Each row of data indicates the values being grouped, along with the summarized values. This is usually an adequate way of displaying data. But sometimes users prefer data in a crosstab format. The crosstab format is one in which groups are broken out into multiple columns. This has the effect of reducing the number of rows a user needs to look through. Crosstab layouts are typically employed by many reporting tools. A prime example of a crosstab layout is the Excel pivot table, which allows you to lay out data in both rows and columns. In this chapter, we'll show how to create this effect with a SQL command.

Adding Subtotals with ROLLUP

In the previous chapter, we showed how to use the GROUP BY clause to group data together. Often when data is grouped together, some columns might be aggregated to provide a sum of values in that column. To revisit this scenario, let's begin with the following data that shows the current inventory of a few products.

InventoryID	Category	Subcategory	Product	Quantity
1	Furniture	Chair	Red Armchair	3
2	Furniture	Chair	Green Armchair	2
3	Furniture	Desk	Blue Computer Desk	4
4	Paper	Copy	White Copy Paper	5
5	Paper	Copy	Pink Copy Paper	2
6	Paper	Notebook	White Notebook Paper	4

In this example, each product is broken down by category and subcategory. For example, the Furniture category includes Chair and Desk subcategories. The following SELECT statement groups this data by Category and Subcategory, and sums the quantity for each group.

```
SELECT
Category,
Subcategory,
SUM(Quantity) AS 'Quantity'
FROM Inventory
GROUP BY Category, Subcategory
ORDER BY Category, Subcategory
```

The resulting output is:

Category	Subcategory	Quantity
Furniture	Chair	5
Furniture	Desk	4
Paper	Copy	7
Paper	Notebook	4

So far, all is well. But what if we also want to see subtotals for each category and a final total at the end? In other words, in addition to the grouped data, we would like a subtotal row every time a category changes, and a final row at the end that sums all the quantities. This can be accomplished by use of a ROLLUP keyword in the GROUP BY clause, as follows:

```
SELECT
Category,
Subcategory,
SUM(Quantity) AS 'Quantity'
FROM Inventory
GROUP BY ROLLUP(Category, Subcategory)
```

The keyword ROLLUP is an extension to the GROUP BY clause that creates subtotal and total rows. The output of the above statement is:

Category	Subcategory	Quantity
Furniture	Chair	5
Furniture	Desk	4
Furniture	NULL	9
Paper	Copy	7
Paper	Notebook	4
Paper	NULL	11
NULL	NULL	20

As seen, three subtotal and total rows have been added to the original four rows. These rows have the keyword NULL in either the Category or Subcategory columns. The first subtotal row is the third row, displaying a quantity of 9 for the Furniture category. The Subcategory is shown as NULL because we are showing only a subtotal for the category. The second of the subtotal rows is the sixth row, which summarizes the Paper category, indicating that there are 11 paper items. The final row is a total column that sums all items in all categories, indicating that we have 20 total items in inventory.

Note that the NULL that appears in the output is somewhat different from the NULL values we've seen previously. In this case, the NULL is merely a placeholder that indicates that a ROLLUP has been applied.

The previous statement did not include an ORDER BY clause. Without an ORDER BY, the subtotal and total rows always appear after each category. Let's now add an ORDER BY to the statement to see the difference:

```
SELECT
Category,
Subcategory,
SUM(Quantity) AS 'Quantity'
FROM Inventory
GROUP BY ROLLUP(Category, Subcategory)
ORDER BY Category, Subcategory
```

The output is:

Category	Subcategory	Quantity
NULL	NULL	20
Furniture	NULL	9
Furniture	Chair	5
Furniture	Desk	4
Paper	NULL	11
Paper	Copy	7
Paper	Notebook	4

As you can see, the ORDER BY clause changes the location of the the subtotal and total rows. They now appear before rather than after each category. This is because NULL values are the lowest possible value, so they appear first in the sorted sequence.

It's plain to see that the use of the NULL values in the above examples is somewhat obtuse and difficult to interpret. We'll now show how to convert those NULL values to something more meaningful. This is accomplished via a function called GROUPING. This is a special aggregate function that works in conjunction with the ROLLUP keyword. As will be seen in the next section, GROUPING also works with the CUBE keyword. The following example adds two columns that make use of the GROUPING function. To make things simpler, we'll remove the ORDER BY clause.

```
SELECT
Category,
Subcategory,
SUM(Quantity) AS 'Quantity',
GROUPING(Category) AS 'Category Grouping',
GROUPING(Subcategory) AS 'Subcategory Grouping'
FROM Inventory
GROUP BY ROLLUP(Category, Subcategory)
```

The output is:

Category	Subcategory	Quantity	Category Grouping	Subcategory Grouping
Furniture	Chair	5	0	0
Furniture	Desk	4	0	0
Furniture	NULL	9	0	1
Paper	Copy	7	0	0
Paper	Notebook	4	0	0
Paper	NULL	11	0	1
NULL	NULL	20	1	1

Let's examine the output to see what the GROUPING function accomplishes. This function has a single argument, which is the name of the column to be examined, and it returns either a 0 or a 1. A 1 means that this row contains a subtotal or total, as specified by the same column in the ROLLUP in the GROUP BY clause. In this example, the ROLLUP is on Category and Subcategory. So the Grouping function on Subcategory returns a 1 if this row provides a subtotal for Subcategory. The function returns a 0 if it is not a subtotal row for the specified column. As you can see, the third row in the preceding output has a NULL in the Subcategory column, and a corresponding value of 1 in the Subcategory Grouping column.

Now that we've see what the GROUPING function does, let's put it to good use. In the next example, we'll introduce a CASE statement to translate the result of the GROUPING function to a more meaningful label.

```
SELECT
ISNULL(Category,'') AS 'Category',
ISNULL(Subcategory, '') AS 'Subcategory',
SUM(Quantity) AS 'Quantity',
CASE WHEN GROUPING(Category) = 1 then 'Grand Total'
WHEN GROUPING(Subcategory) = 1 then 'Subtotal'
ELSE ' ' END AS 'Subtotal/Total'
FROM Inventory
GROUP BY ROLLUP(Category, Subcategory)
```

This produces the following output:

Category	Subcategory	Quantity	Subtotal/Total
Furniture	Chair	5	
Furniture	Desk	4	
Furniture		9	Subtotal
Paper	Copy	7	
Paper	Notebook	4	
Paper		11	Subtotal
		20	Grand Total

The ISNULL function in the Category and Subcategory columns suppresses the printing of the word NULL. The CASE statement in the new Subtotal/Total column uses the GROUPING function to print either "Subtotal" or "Grand Total" in the column if the Quantity is a Subtotal or Grand Total.

There's still more that can be done to make the display a little more understandable. In the following example, we've moved the CASE statement to the first column.

```
SELECT
CASE
WHEN GROUPING(Category) = 1 THEN 'GRAND TOTAL'
WHEN GROUPING(Subcategory) = 1 THEN 'SUBTOTAL'
ELSE ISNULL(Category,'') END AS 'Category',
ISNULL(Subcategory, '') AS 'Subcategory',
SUM(Quantity) AS 'Quantity'
FROM Inventory
GROUP BY ROLLUP(Category, Subcategory)
```

Now the output is:

Category	Subcategory	Quantity
Furniture	Chair	5
Furniture	Desk	4
SUBTOTAL		9
Paper	Copy	7
Paper	Notebook	4
SUBTOTAL		11
GRAND TOTAL		20

As seen, the CASE statement under the Category column prints the words SUBTOTAL or TOTAL, if the corresponding quantity is a subtotal or total. The GROUPING function is used to make this determination.

> ### Database Differences: MySQL
>
> MySQL has a slightly different format for the ROLLUP keyword. The equivalent of this SQL Server line:
>
> ```
> GROUP BY ROLLUP(Category, Subcategory)
> ```
>
> in MySQL is:
>
> ```
> GROUP BY Category, Subcategory WITH ROLLUP
> ```
>
> MySQL doesn't allow an ORDER BY clause if WITH ROLLUP is used. Also, MySQL doesn't support the GROUPING function.

Adding Subtotals with CUBE

Rollups work well in situations where the data has a hierarchical structure. In the previous example, there was a natural hierarchy from category to subcategory. As such, you can think of drilling down from category to subcategory. The ROLLUP keyword provides subtotals on each category and a total at the end.

However, there are other situations in which the data is not hierarchical, but where we still want to add subtotal rows. To illustrate that scenario, let's look at the following data.

SalesDate	CustomerID	State	Channel	SalesAmount
4/1/2017	101	NY	Internet	50
4/1/2017	102	NY	Retail	30
4/1/2017	103	VT	Internet	120
4/2/2017	145	VT	Retail	90
4/2/2017	180	NY	Retail	300
4/2/2017	181	VT	Internet	130
4/2/2017	182	NY	Internet	520
4/2/2017	184	NY	Retail	80

This data shows sales by customer and date, indicating the state and channel of the sale. In this example, there are only two states, NY and VT, and two channels, Internet and retail. Let's say that we're interested in learning total sales by state and channel. Even though we have sales from multiple customers on multiple dates, we don't have a need to aggregate by customer or date at this moment. We can view total sales by state and channel with this statement:

```
SELECT
State,
Channel,
SUM(SalesAmount) AS 'Sales Amount'
FROM SalesSummary
GROUP BY State, Channel
ORDER BY State, Channel
```

The resulting output is:

State	Channel	Sales Amount
NY	Internet	570
NY	Retail	410
VT	Internet	250
VT	Retail	90

So far, we've applied only a simple GROUP BY to obtain the aggregated sales amounts for each combination of state and channel. Now, let's say that we want to see subtotal and total rows, similar to what we did previously with the furniture inventory data. The problem we face is that there isn't a natural hierarchy between state and channel, as there was between category and subcategory. If we're using subtotals, there's no obvious way to indicate how the subtotals are to be calculated. In effect, we want to see subtotals for both state and channel, independent of each other.

To accomplish this, we'll use a new keyword, CUBE, similar to how we previously used ROLLUP. The following statement produces the desired result:

```
SELECT
State,
Channel,
SUM(SalesAmount) AS 'Sales Amount'
FROM SalesSummary
GROUP BY CUBE(State, Channel)
ORDER BY State, Channel
```

The output is:

State	Channel	Sales Amount
NULL	NULL	1320
NULL	Internet	820
NULL	Retail	500
NY	NULL	980
NY	Internet	570
NY	Retail	410
VT	NULL	340
VT	Internet	250
VT	Retail	90

As with the previous example, the NULL values in the State and Channel columns indicate a subtotal or a grand total. The first row, with NULL values in both State and Channel is a grand total for all the data. The second and third rows, with NULL in the State column, show subtotals for the Channel column. For example, the second row indicates that there was a total of 820 in Internet sales. The fourth and seventh rows, with NULL in the Channel column, have subtotals for the State column. As seen, NY had a total of 980 in sales, and VT had 340 in sales.

The use of the keyword CUBE is meant to express a multidimensional way of looking at the data. Whereas the ROLLUP keyword lets you drill down through data in a hierarchical fashion, the CUBE keyword allows for multiple dimensions. In this example, we can view subtotals by State or by Column.

As before, identifying the subtotals and grand totals is tricky. Ideally, you want to eliminate all of the NULL values and indicate more precisely which rows are subtotals and grand totals. As with rollups, we can use the GROUPING function to determine which rows are subtotals. The following query adds two columns with the GROUPING information.

```
SELECT
State,
Channel,
SUM(SalesAmount) AS 'Sales Amount',
GROUPING(State) AS 'State Grouping',
GROUPING(Channel) AS 'Channel Grouping'
FROM SalesSummary
GROUP BY CUBE(State, Channel)
ORDER BY State, Channel
```

The output of this is:

State	Channel	Sales Amount	State Grouping	Channel Grouping
NULL	NULL	1320	1	1
NULL	Internet	820	1	0
NULL	Retail	500	1	0
NY	NULL	980	0	1
NY	Internet	570	0	0
NY	Retail	410	0	0
VT	NULL	340	0	1
VT	Internet	250	0	0
VT	Retail	90	0	0

We're still not at a point where the output makes sense, but now we're going to get clever and use the GROUPING function, along with a few other tricks, to make this output more presentable. We'll execute the following statement, and then explain it after we've seen the output.

```
SELECT
ISNULL(State,' ') AS 'State',
ISNULL(Channel, ' ') AS 'Channel',
SUM(SalesAmount) AS 'Sales Amount',
CASE WHEN GROUPING(State) = 1
AND GROUPING(Channel) = 1 THEN 'Grand Total'
WHEN GROUPING(State) = 1
AND GROUPING(Channel) = 0 THEN 'Channel Subtotal'
WHEN GROUPING(State) = 0
AND GROUPING(Channel) = 1 THEN 'State Subtotal'
ELSE ' ' END AS 'Subtotal/Total'
FROM SalesSummary
GROUP BY CUBE(State, Channel)
ORDER BY
CASE
WHEN GROUPING(State) = 0 AND GROUPING(Channel) = 0 THEN 1
WHEN GROUPING(State) = 0 AND GROUPING(Channel) = 1 THEN 2
WHEN GROUPING(State) = 1 AND GROUPING(Channel) = 0 THEN 3
ELSE 4
END
```

The output is:

State	Channel	Sales Amount	Subtotal/Total
NY	Retail	410	
VT	Retail	90	
NY	Internet	570	
VT	Internet	250	
NY		980	State Subtotal
VT		340	State Subtotal
	Internet	820	Channel Subtotal
	Retail	500	Channel Subtotal
		1320	Grand Total

Let's pause now to discuss how this output was produced. The first column uses a CASE statement to print the State label only if the row is not for a subtotal or grand total. Similarly, the second column does the same for the Channel label. The third column uses a SUM function to print the sales amount for that row. The fourth column uses a CASE statement to produce the Subtotal/Total label. As you can see, the CASE uses the GROUPING function to determine whether this is a State subtotal, a Channel subtotal, or a grand total. If it's none of those, SQL prints a blank in that column. The GROUP BY clause uses the CUBE keyword to create subtotals for all of the combinations specified. Finally, we've used a CASE statement and the GROUPING function in the ORDER BY clause to make sure that the subtotals appear after the detail rows, and the grand total row appears at the very end.

Database Differences: MySQL

MySQL doesn't support the CUBE keyword.

Creating Crosstab Layouts

The subtotal rows added with the ROLLUP and CUBE keywords provide additional aggregation possibilities for your queries. By displaying additional subtotal rows, we can view summary information along with the details. We now want to turn our attention to the way that summarized data is typically presented. We already encountered this statement that groups data by state and channel to provide an aggregated summary:

```
SELECT
State,
Channel,
SUM(SalesAmount) AS 'Sales Amount'
FROM SalesSummary
GROUP BY State, Channel
ORDER BY State, Channel
```

The output is:

State	Channel	Sales Amount
NY	Internet	570
NY	Retail	410
VT	Internet	250
VT	Retail	90

This data is perfectly understandable. We have four rows of data, in which each row gives an aggregated summary of a specific state and channel combination. For example, the first row provides the sum of sales over the Internet in NY. This is all well and good, but we now want to introduce an alternate way of displaying this same information. Using a new keyword called PIVOT, it's possible to display this data as it would appear in an Excel pivot table, in what is commonly called a *crosstab query*. Using the PIVOT keyword, we can produce this output in the following layout:

Channel	NY	VT
Internet	570	250
Retail	410	90

Instead of four rows of data, we now have only two. This was accomplished by breaking down the state values into separate columns. This compact way of displaying data is referred to as a *crosstab*. If you're familiar with Microsoft Excel, this is similar to what is seen in Excel pivot tables. We'll discuss pivot tables in Chapter 20, but for now the main idea to remember is that pivot tables divide columns into four distinct areas: rows, columns, filters, and values. If this were a pivot table, we would have placed Channel in the rows area, State in the columns area, and Sales Amount in the values area.

The virtue of the crosstab is that it is more compact and makes it easier to navigate through the data. For example, if we're interested in finding retail sales in VT, we simply locate the Retail row and VT column and then find the intersection. With the traditional aggregated summary, we would need to scan the various rows until we locate the row with the desired Channel and State values.

Let's now see how the above crosstab output was accomplished. A query that creates this output is:

```
SELECT * FROM
(SELECT Channel, State, SalesAmount FROM SalesSummary) AS mainquery
PIVOT (SUM(SalesAmount) FOR State IN ([NY], [VT])) AS pivotquery
```

This is quite a bit more complex than anything we've seen previously. In a way, this is like combining two queries together—a topic that will be discussed in Chapters 13 and 14. In order to decipher this, we'll need to break down the statement into its components. The portion of the second line of the query that's within parentheses is:

```
SELECT
Channel,
State,
SalesAmount
FROM SalesSummary
```

This query selects all data for the three columns of interest in the SalesSummary table. The AS keyword that follows is used to provide an alias for the entire query. In this case, we're calling it *mainquery*, which is an arbitrary name; we could have called it anything.

The third line introduces the PIVOT operator. This keyword indicates that we will pivot on the data items that follow. This means that we want data to appear in a crosstab format. The first item listed is always an aggregation function. In this example, it is:

```
SUM(SalesAmount)
```

This indicates that we want to sum values in the SalesAmount column. The FOR keyword that follows separates the aggregation function from the field that we want to appear as separate columns in the pivot table. In this example, we want values for State to appear as separate columns. The IN keyword separates the column name from the values that we want to appear as column headers. The PIVOT operator requires us to explicitly state the values we want as column headers. In this example, those values are NY and VT. Note that SQL Server requires that these enumerated values be enclosed in brackets rather than the normal single quotes. Finally, we assign an alias to the entire PIVOT expression, which in this example is *pivotquery*. Like the *mainquery* alias, this is an entirely arbitrary name.

To recap, we've seen that this statement has this general structure:

```
SELECT * FROM
(a SELECT query that produces the data) AS alias_for_source_query
PIVOT (aggregation_function(column)
FOR column_for_column_headers
IN pivot_column_values)
AS alias_for_pivot_table
```

It might first appear that this was a lot of unnecessary extra work to produce a result that's not significantly more useful than the original output. To better illustrate the value of the PIVOT operator, let's now add another level of aggregation, the sales date, into the mix. Going back to non-crosstab queries, we can run this variation of the original query:

```
SELECT
SalesDate,
State,
Channel,
SUM(SalesAmount) AS Total
FROM SalesSummary
GROUP BY SalesDate, State, Channel
ORDER BY SalesDate, State, Channel
```

As you can see, we have added SalesDate to the GROUP BY and ORDER BY clauses. The output is:

SalesDate	State	Channel	Total
2017-04-01	NY	Internet	50
2017-04-01	NY	Retail	30
2017-04-01	VT	Internet	120
2017-04-02	NY	Internet	520
2017-04-02	NY	Retail	380
2017-04-02	VT	Internet	130
2017-04-02	VT	Retail	90

With an increased number of rows, this is a bit more difficult to interpret. For example, if we want to find the retail sales for NY on 4/2/2017, we'll have to scan the rows until we find that the fifth row provides this information. Moreover, if we want to find retail sales from VT on 4/1/2017, it might take some time to realize that there are no rows with that information. This is because our underlying data had no retail sales from VT on 4/1/2017.

Using the PIVOT operator, we can produce this same data in a crosstab layout, making it easier to locate the desired data points. Our objective is to produce the data in this format:

SalesDate	Channel	NY	VT
2017-04-01	Internet	50	120
2017-04-01	Retail	30	NULL
2017-04-02	Internet	520	130
2017-04-02	Retail	380	90

This can be accomplished with the following PIVOT statement:

```
SELECT * FROM
(SELECT SalesDate, Channel, State, SalesAmount FROM SalesSummary)
AS mainquery
PIVOT (SUM(SalesAmount) FOR State IN ([NY], [VT])) AS pivotquery
ORDER BY SalesDate
```

We've made only two changes to the previous PIVOT statement. First, we added the SalesDate as a selected column in the *mainquery* portion of the statement. Second, we added an ORDER BY clause, which causes the rows to be sorted by date. Unlike before, we now have both the

SalesDate and Channel fields in the rows area of the crosstab. The columns area still has the state, with each state listed in a separate column.

Notice that we see a NULL value for retail sales for VT on 4/1/2017. This explicitly tells us that we had no such sales. This is a vast improvement over the traditional display of data, where it is more difficult to determine that fact.

Also note that the order of fields in the mainquery SELECT is significant. In the query, we have SalesDate listed before Channel. This caused the SalesDate column to appear to the left of the Channel column. We could have easily switched the order of those two columns, as in the following:

```
SELECT * FROM
(SELECT Channel, SalesDate, State, SalesAmount FROM SalesSummary) AS mainquery
PIVOT (SUM(SalesAmount) FOR State IN ([NY], [VT])) AS pivotquery
ORDER BY Channel
```

We also modified the column specified in the ORDER BY clause. The resulting output is:

Channel	SalesDate	NY	VT
Internet	2017-04-01	50	120
Internet	2017-04-02	520	130
Retail	2017-04-01	30	NULL
Retail	2017-04-02	380	90

As you can see, the resulting output is somewhat different but has the same information.

Once you have more than two data elements in a crosstab query, there are many ways to arrange the data. For example, we could have have chosen to put the Channel in the columns area rather than the State. This would look like:

SalesDate	State	Internet	Retail
2017-04-01	NY	50	30
2017-04-01	VT	120	NULL
2017-04-02	NY	520	380
2017-04-02	VT	130	90

The statement that produces this layout is:

```
SELECT * FROM
(SELECT SalesDate, State, Channel, SalesAmount FROM SalesSummary) AS mainquery
PIVOT (SUM(SalesAmount) FOR Channel IN ([Internet], [Retail])) AS pivotquery
ORDER BY SalesDate
```

The main change in this query is that we've specified Channel values in the *pivotquery* portion of the statement. This causes the Channel values, Internet and Retail, to be broken out as separate columns in the display.

Remember that one of the main difficulties with using the PIVOT command is that all column values must be explicitly listed. If you're querying data, you must know what these values are in advance of writing the query. For small categorical data items, this may not be a problem. But for data where there are many possible values that can change over time, this can be problematic. In Chapter 20, "Strategies for Displaying Data," we'll discuss an alternative to PIVOT crosstab queries—namely, Excel pivot tables. Unlike crosstab queries, pivot tables do not require the user to know in advance what values will appear. Pivot tables display rows and columns dynamically, as needed, based on the values that are present. Hence, it is often more expedient to give the user raw data and let them create a crosstab layout via Excel pivot tables.

> ### Database Differences: MySQL and Oracle
>
> MySQL doesn't support the PIVOT keyword.
>
> Oracle uses slightly different syntax for the PIVOT keyword. The equivalent of this SQL Server statement:
>
> ```
> SELECT * FROM
> (SELECT Channel, State, SalesAmount FROM SalesSummary) AS mainquery
> PIVOT (SUM(SalesAmount) FOR State IN ([NY], [VT])) AS pivotquery
> ```
>
> in Oracle is:
>
> ```
> SELECT * FROM
> (SELECT Channel, State, SalesAmount FROM SalesSummary)
> PIVOT (SUM(SalesAmount) FOR State IN ('NY', 'VT'));
> ```
>
> Unlike SQL Server, Oracle uses quotes rather than brackets for the enumerated values and does not use aliases (mainquery and pivotquery in this example).

Looking Ahead

This chapter took a slight detour into matters concerning layout. The ROLLUP and CUBE keywords allow the GROUPING clause to generate additional subtotal rows on any number of columns. The ROLLUP keyword works best with data for which there is a clear hierarchy among the columns. In our example, there was a hierarchical relationship between the Category and Subcategory columns of the Inventory table. In contrast, the CUBE keyword generates all combinations of subtotals for the specified columns. As with a cube structure, subtotals can be viewed from any perspective. We also discussed the GROUPING function, which provides a way to add clarity to subtotal displays.

Our second topic in this chapter, crosstabs, used the PIVOT operator to produce data in a useful crosstab layout. Although PIVOT queries are somewhat cumbersome to create, they sometimes serve a purpose in generating data in a comprehensible format for the end user. In Chapter 20, we'll discuss Excel pivot tables, which are usually an easier way to display data in a crosstab fashion.

In our next chapter, "Inner Joins," we'll return from this detour to rejoin the main focus of this book. Up until now, all of our queries have involved retrieving data from one table at a time. The next few chapters will explore methods of combining data from multiple tables at once. In the real world of computing, required data seldom comes from a single table. Thus, it is essential to learn how to relate and combine data from more than one table in a single query.

11

Inner Joins

Keywords Introduced

INNER JOIN · ON

Back in Chapter 1, we talked about the huge advance of relational databases over their predecessors. The significant achievement of relational databases was in their ability to allow data to be organized in any number of tables that are related but at the same time independent of each other. Prior to the advent of relational databases, traditional databases utilized a chain of internal pointers to explicitly define the relationships between tables. For example, you might start with a Customers table and then follow pointers to find the first order for a particular customer, then the next order, and so on until all orders for the customer have been retrieved. In contrast, relational databases allow relationships to be inferred by columns that tables have in common. These relationships are sometimes formalized by the definition of primary and foreign keys, but that isn't always necessary.

With relational databases, it is the responsibility of the SQL developer to determine and define the relationships between tables. This allows for great flexibility in how different data elements can be combined. The great virtue of relational databases lies in the fact that someone can grab data from a variety of tables in ways that serve the immediate business requirement.

Let's start with a common example. Most organizations have a business entity known as a *customer*. As such, a database typically contains a Customers table that defines each customer. Such a table would normally include a primary key to uniquely identify each customer, and any number of columns with attributes that further define the customer. Common attributes might include phone number, address, city, state, and so on.

The main idea is that all information about the customer is stored in a single table and only in that table. This simplifies the task of data updates. When a customer changes his phone number, only one table needs to be updated. However, the downside to this setup is that whenever someone needs any information about a customer, they must access the Customers table to retrieve the data.

This brings us to the concept of a *join*. Let's say that someone is analyzing products that have been purchased. Along with information about the products, it might be necessary to provide information about the customers who purchased each product. For example, an analyst may wish to obtain customer ZIP codes for a geographic analysis. Whereas product information may be found in a Products table, the ZIP code is stored only in the Customers table. To get information on both customers and products, the analyst must join both tables together in such a way that the data matches correctly.

In essence, the promise of relational databases is fulfilled by the ability to join tables together in any desired manner. This is the normal situation. With this chapter, we will leave behind the somewhat artificial examples for which data is retrieved only from a single table and encounter more realistic scenarios involving data in multiple tables.

Joining Two Tables

To begin our exploration of the join process, let's revisit the Sales table that we encountered previously in Chapters 3 and 6:

SalesID	FirstName	LastName	QuantityPurchased	PricePerItem
1	Andrew	Li	4	2.50
2	Carol	White	10	1.25
3	James	Carpenter	5	4.00

To some extent, the use of this table in earlier chapters was somewhat misleading. In reality, a competent database designer would seldom create a table such as this. The problem is that it contains information about two separate entities, customers and orders. In the real world, this information would be split into at least two separate tables. A Customers table might look like the following table, seen previously in Chapter 2, "Basic Data Retrieval":

CustomerID	FirstName	LastName
1	Sara	Davis
2	Rumi	Shah
3	Paul	Johnson
4	Samuel	Martinez

An Orders table might look like this:

OrderID	CustomerID	OrderDate	OrderAmount
1	1	2016-09-01	10.00
2	2	2016-09-02	12.50
3	2	2016-09-03	18.00
4	3	2016-09-15	20.00

In this Orders table, we've chosen to include OrderDate and OrderAmount columns, rather than the QuantityPurchased and PricePerItem columns seen in the first Sales table. Notice that the data that was in the Sales table has now been split into two separate tables. The Customers table contains information only about customers. The Orders table contains information solely about items purchased. The Orders table includes a CustomerID column to indicate which customer placed the order. As you might remember from Chapter 1, "Relational Databases and SQL," this is referred to as a *foreign key*.

Even though the Customers and Orders tables both have four rows, this is something of a coincidence. There is one customer in the Customers table who has not placed an order. As you can see, CustomerID 4, Samuel Martinez, does not appear in the Orders table. On the other hand, Rumi Shah has placed two different orders, as evidenced by the two rows in the Orders table with an CustomerID of 2.

Even with these two tables, there is still much missing. For example, an Orders table would typically include additional columns, such as information on the tax collected or the salesperson's name. Plus, the Orders table itself might in fact be split into more than one table so that information about the entire order, such as the order date, could be stored apart from information about each item that was ordered. In other words, this is still not a completely realistic example. However, now that we've split our information into two separate tables, we can address how to create a SELECT statement that can pull data from both tables simultaneously.

Before we get to the SELECT statement itself, we need to address one additional concern, which is how to visually represent the two tables and the implied relationship that exists between them. Previously, we displayed each table with column names on the top row and corresponding data on subsequent rows. Now that we have more than one table to deal with, we'll introduce another type of visual representation. Figure 11.1 shows a diagram with both tables, with the table name on the top row and the column names in each subsequent row. This diagram is a simplified version of what is commonly called an *entity-relationship* diagram. The term *entity* refers to the tables, and *relationship* refers to the line drawn between the data elements in those tables. Rather than showing detailed data, this diagram indicates the overall structure of the data.

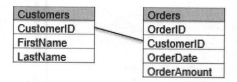

Figure 11.1   Entity-relationship diagram

The important point to notice is that we've drawn a line from CustomerID in the Customers table to the CustomerID in the Orders table. This indicates a relationship between these two tables—namely, that both tables share values stored in the CustomerID column.

The Inner Join

We are now ready to present a SELECT statement with what is called an *inner join*:

```
SELECT *
FROM Customers
INNER JOIN Orders
ON Customers.CustomerID = Orders.CustomerID
```

Let's examine this statement line by line. The SELECT keyword on the first line merely states that we want all (*) columns from both tables. The second line, with the FROM clause, indicates that the first table we want to specify is the Customers table. The third line introduces the new INNER JOIN keyword. This keyword is used to specify an additional table that we want to include in our query. In this case, we want to add the Orders table.

Finally, the fourth line introduces the ON keyword. This ON works in conjunction with the INNER JOIN and specifies exactly how the two tables are to be joined. In this case, we are connecting the CustomerID column of the Customers table (Customers.CustomerID) to the CustomerID column of the Orders table (Orders.CustomerID). Because the CustomerID column has the same name in both the Customers and Orders table, we need to specify the table name as a prefix to the CustomerID column name. The prefix allows us to distinguish between these columns in two separate tables.

The preceding SELECT statement produces this data:

CustomerID	FirstName	LastName	OrderID	CustomerID	OrderDate	OrderAmount
1	Sara	Davis	1	1	2016-09-01	10.00
2	Rumi	Shah	2	2	2016-09-02	12.50
2	Rumi	Shah	3	2	2016-09-03	18.00
3	Paul	Johnson	4	3	2016-09-15	20.00

Let's analyze the results. Both the Customers table and the Orders table had four rows. Looking at the OrderID column, you can tell that we have data from all four rows from the Orders table. However, looking at the CustomerID column, you might notice that only three customers are shown. Why is that? The answer is that the customer with a CustomerID of 4 doesn't exist in the Orders table. Because we're joining the two tables together on the CustomerID field, we have no rows in the Orders table that match the CustomerID of 4 in the Customers table.

This brings us to an important observation: An inner join only returns data for which there is a match between both tables being joined. In the next chapter, we'll talk about an alternative method of joining tables that will allow the customer information for the CustomerID of 4 to be shown, even if there are no orders for that customer.

Here's a second important observation: Notice that the customer data for Rumi Shah is repeated twice. She existed only once in the Customers table, so one might wonder why she appears on two rows. The answer is that the INNER JOIN causes all possible matches to be shown. Because Rumi has two rows in the Orders table, both of these rows match with her row in the Customers table, resulting in her customer information being displayed twice.

Finally, you may be wondering why this join is referred to an inner join. There are, in fact, two main variations of the join: the inner join and the outer join. Outer joins will be covered in the next chapter.

Table Order in Inner Joins

An inner join brings back data where there is a match between the two specified tables. In the previous SELECT, we specified the Customers table in the FROM clause and the Orders table in the INNER JOIN clause. We might ask whether it matters which table is specified first. As it turns out, for inner joins, the order in which the tables are listed can be reversed with no difference in the results. The following two SELECT statements are logically identical and return the same data:

```
SELECT *
FROM Customers
INNER JOIN Orders
ON Customers.CustomerID = Orders.CustomerID

SELECT *
FROM Orders
INNER JOIN Customers
ON Orders.CustomerID = Customers.CustomerID
```

The only difference is that the first statement would display columns from the Customers table first and the Orders table second. The second statement would display columns from the Orders table first and the Customers table second. Despite the order of the columns, both statements return identical data.

Remember that SQL is not a procedural language. It doesn't specify how a task is to be completed. SQL only indicates the desired logic, and leaves it to the internals of the database to decide exactly how to perform the required task. As such, SQL doesn't determine how the database physically retrieves data. It doesn't define which table to physically look at first. Instead, the database software determines the optimal method of obtaining the data.

An Alternate Specification of Inner Joins

In the previous examples, we used the INNER JOIN and ON keywords to specify inner joins. It is also possible to specify inner joins with just the FROM and WHERE clauses. We have already seen this statement that joins the Customers and Orders tables:

```
SELECT *
FROM Customers
INNER JOIN Orders
ON Customers.CustomerID = Orders.CustomerID
```

An alternate way of specifying the same inner join without the INNER JOIN and ON keywords is:

```
SELECT *
FROM Customers, Orders
WHERE Customers.CustomerID = Orders.CustomerID
```

In this alternate specification, rather than using the INNER JOIN keyword to define the new table to join to, we merely list all tables to be joined in the FROM clause. Instead of using the ON clause to say how the tables are related, we use the WHERE clause to specify the relationship between the tables.

Even though this alternate format works perfectly well and produces the same results, we don't recommend its use. The advantage of the INNER JOIN and ON keywords is that they explicitly present the logic of the join. That is their only purpose. Although it is possible to specify the relationship in a WHERE clause, the meaning of the SQL statement is less obvious when the WHERE clause is used for selection criteria and also to indicate relationships between multiple tables.

Table Aliases Revisited

Let's now look at the columns that were returned from the previous SELECT statement. Because we specified all (*) columns, we see all columns from both tables. The CustomerID column appears twice because that column exists in both tables. In practice, however, we would not want this data repeated. Here's an alternate version of the SELECT, which now specifies only the columns we want to see. In this variant, we employ table aliases, C for Customers and O for Orders, which are placed immediately after the FROM and INNER JOIN keywords by inserting the AS keyword. The statement looks like this:

```
SELECT
C.CustomerID AS 'Cust ID',
C.FirstName AS 'First Name',
C.LastName AS 'Last Name',
O.OrderID AS 'Order ID',
O.OrderDate AS 'Date',
O.OrderAmount AS 'Amount'
FROM Customers AS C
INNER JOIN Orders AS O
ON C.CustomerID = O.CustomerID
```

The results are:

Cust ID	First Name	Last Name	Order ID	Date	Amount
1	Sara	Davis	1	2016-09-01	10.00
2	Rumi	Shah	2	2016-09-02	12.50
2	Rumi	Shah	3	2016-09-03	18.00
3	Paul	Johnson	4	2016-09-15	20.00

In this statement, we're displaying only the CustomerID from the Customers table, and not from the Orders table. Also notice that we're using the AS keyword to specify both column and table aliases. Note that the AS keyword is completely optional. All of the AS keywords can be removed from this SELECT, and the statement would still be valid and return the same results. However, we recommend using the AS keywords for the sake of clarity.

Database Differences: Oracle

As mentioned in Chapter 3, "Calculated Fields and Aliases," table aliases are specified in Oracle without the AS keyword. The syntax for the equivalent statement in Oracle is:

```
SELECT
C.CustomerID AS "Cust ID",
C.FirstName AS "First Name",
C.LastName AS "Last Name",
O.OrderID AS "Order ID",
O.OrderDate AS "Date",
O.OrderAmount AS "Amount"
FROM Customers C
INNER JOIN Orders O
ON C.CustomerID = O.CustomerID;
```

Although we see the AS keyword used for column aliases, the AS keyword is not used for table aliases in Oracle.

Looking Ahead

The ability to join tables together in a query is an essential feature of SQL. Relational databases would be of little use without joins. This chapter focused on the formulation of the inner join. The inner join brings back data for which there is a match between both tables being joined. We also talked about an alternate way of specifying the inner join, and the usefulness of using table aliases.

In our next chapter, we will turn to another important type of join: the outer join. As mentioned, inner joins only allow us to view data where there is a match between the tables being joined. So, if you have a customer with no orders, you won't see any customer information when doing an inner join between a Customers table and an Orders table. The outer join will allow you to view that customer information, even if there are no orders for the customer. In other words, the outer join lets us see data that we would not otherwise be able to obtain with an inner join. Additionally, the next chapter will begin introducing scenarios in which more than two tables are joined.

12

Outer Joins

Keywords Introduced

LEFT JOIN · RIGHT JOIN · FULL JOIN · CROSS JOIN

We now advance from inner joins to outer joins. The main restriction of inner joins is that they require a match in all tables being joined to show any results. If you're joining a Customers table to an Orders table, no data is shown for the customer if that customer hasn't yet placed an order. This may seem like a relatively unimportant problem, but it often becomes significant with different types of data.

To use a different example, let's say we have an Orders table and a Refunds table. The Refunds table is related to the Orders table by OrderID. In other words, all refunds are tied to a specific order. The refund can't exist unless the order exists. The problem arises when we want to see both orders and refunds in a single query. If we join these two tables with an inner join, we won't see any orders if no refunds were issued against that order. Presumably, this would be the majority of the orders. The outer join allows us to view orders even if they don't have a matching refund, and is therefore an essential technique to understand and use.

The Outer Join

All the joins seen in the previous chapter were inner joins. Because inner joins are the most common join type, SQL considers them the default join. You can specify an inner join using only the keyword JOIN; it isn't necessary to state INNER JOIN.

In contrast to inner joins, there are three types of outer joins: LEFT OUTER JOIN, RIGHT OUTER JOIN, and FULL OUTER JOIN. These can be referred to as simply LEFT JOIN, RIGHT JOIN, and FULL JOIN. In this case, the word OUTER isn't necessary. To summarize, our recommendation is to refer to the four join types as:

- INNER JOIN
- LEFT JOIN
- RIGHT JOIN
- FULL JOIN

This keeps the syntax simple and consistent. At the end of this chapter, we'll also briefly illustrate something called the CROSS JOIN, but that join is neither an inner nor an outer join and is seldom used.

We'll use three tables in our examples of outer joins. The first will be a Customers table with information about each customer. The second will be an Orders table with data on each order placed. We'll reference Customers and Orders tables with the same data seen in the previous chapter. Finally, we'll add a Refunds table with information about any refunds that have been issued to customers.

Figure 12.1 shows how these three tables are related.

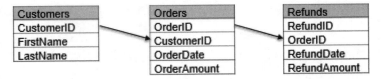

Figure 12.1   Entity-relationship diagram for three tables

In contrast to the figure seen in the previous chapter, the lines connecting the tables are now shown as arrows. For example, the arrow drawn from the CustomerID field of the Customers table to the CustomerID field of the Orders table indicates that the link between the Customers and Orders table is possibly one-sided, in the sense that there may not be any orders for a given customer. Additionally, there may be multiple orders for a single customer. Similarly, the arrow drawn between the Orders and Refunds tables indicates that there may not be any refunds for a given order, and that there may be multiple refunds for an order.

The line between the Customers and Orders table connects the CustomerID columns because that is the common link between the two tables. Similarly, the line between the Orders and Refunds tables is on the OrderID column because the OrderID is the common link between those two tables.

In other words, the Orders table is related to the Customers table by customer. There must be a customer for an order to exist. The Refunds table is related to the Orders table by the order. There must be an order before a refund is issued. Note that the Refunds table is not directly related to the Customers table; those two tables don't share a common field. However, by joining all three tables together, we will be able to determine which customer a given refund is for.

Let's now examine the contents of each table. The Customers table has these values:

CustomerID	FirstName	LastName
1	Sara	Davis
2	Rumi	Shah
3	Paul	Johnson
4	Samuel	Martinez

The Orders table has these values:

OrderID	CustomerID	OrderDate	OrderAmount
1	1	2016-09-01	10.00
2	2	2016-09-02	12.50
3	2	2016-09-03	18.00
4	3	2016-09-15	20.00

The Refunds table has these values:

RefundID	OrderID	RefundDate	RefundAmount
1	1	2016-09-02	5.00
2	3	2016-09-18	18.00

Notice that only three out of the four customers have placed orders. Likewise, only two refunds have been issued for the four orders placed.

Left Joins

Let's now create a SELECT statement that joins all three tables together using a LEFT JOIN:

```
SELECT
Customers.FirstName AS 'First Name',
Customers.LastName AS 'Last Name',
Orders.OrderDate AS 'Order Date',
Orders.OrderAmount AS 'Order Amt',
Refunds.RefundDate AS 'Refund Date',
Refunds.RefundAmount AS 'Refund Amt'
FROM Customers
LEFT JOIN Orders
ON Customers.CustomerID = Orders.CustomerID
LEFT JOIN Refunds
ON Orders.OrderID = Refunds.OrderID
ORDER BY Customers.LastName, Customers.FirstName, Orders.OrderDate
```

The resulting data looks like:

First Name	Last Name	Order Date	Order Amt	Refund Date	Refund Amt
Sara	Davis	2016-09-01	10.00	2016-09-02	5.00
Paul	Johnson	2016-09-15	20.00	NULL	NULL
Samuel	Martinez	NULL	NULL	NULL	NULL
Rumi	Shah	2016-09-02	12.50	NULL	NULL
Rumi	Shah	2016-09-03	18.00	2016-09-18	18.00

> ### Database Differences: Oracle
>
> Unlike SQL Server and MySQL, Oracle typically displays dates in a DD-MMM-YY format. For example, the date 2016-09-02 in the previous table will display as 02-SEP-16 in Oracle. However, no matter which database you're using, the exact format in which dates are displayed will vary, depending on how your database was set up.

Before analyzing the previous SELECT statement, notice two interesting aspects of the data. First, Samuel Martinez has no data shown other than his name. The reason for the lack of data is that there are no rows in the Orders table associated with that customer. The power of the outer join becomes evident from the fact that we can see some data for Samuel Martinez, even if he has no orders. If we had specified an INNER JOIN rather than a LEFT JOIN, we would see no rows at all for Samuel.

Similarly, there is no refund data for either the 9/2/2016 order from Rumi Shah or the order from Paul Johnson. This is because there are no rows in the Refunds table associated with these orders. If we had specified an INNER JOIN rather than a LEFT JOIN, we would have seen no rows at all for those two orders.

Let's now examine the SELECT statement itself. The first few lines that specify the columns are nothing we haven't seen before. Notice that rather than using table aliases, we've chosen to list all the columns with their fully qualified names, including the table names as a prefix.

The first table listed is the Customers table. This table is shown after the FROM keyword. The second table shown is the Orders table, which appears after the first LEFT JOIN keyword. The subsequent ON clause specifies how the Orders table is linked to the Customers table. The third table shown is the Refunds table, which appears after the second LEFT JOIN keyword. The subsequent ON clause states how the Refunds table is joined to the Orders table.

It is critical to realize that the order in which tables are listed in reference to the LEFT JOIN keyword is significant. When specifying a LEFT JOIN, the table to the left of LEFT JOIN is always the *primary* table. The table to the right of LEFT JOIN is the *secondary* table. When joining the secondary table to the primary table, we want all rows in the primary table, even if there are no matches with any rows in the secondary table.

In the first specified LEFT JOIN, the Customers table is on the left and the Orders table is on the right of the LEFT JOIN. This signifies that Customers is primary and Orders is secondary. In other words, we want to see all selected data from the Customers table, even if there isn't a corresponding match in the secondary table for that row.

Similarly, in the second LEFT JOIN, the Orders table is to the left and the Refunds table is to the right of the LEFT JOIN keyword. That means that we are specifying Orders as primary and Refunds as secondary in this join. We want all orders, even if there are no matching refunds for some orders.

Just as with inner joins, data from one table can be repeated if there is more than one matching row between that table and the table to which it is joined. In this example, we have more than one order for Rumi Shah, so the customer information for Rumi Shah is repeated on two separate lines.

Finally, we included an ORDER BY clause. This was done merely to present the data in an understandable order.

Testing for NULL Values

In the previous SELECT, we had one customer with no orders and two orders with no associated refunds. Unlike the INNER JOIN, the LEFT JOIN allows these rows with missing values to appear.

To test our understanding of the LEFT JOIN, let's now look at how we would list only those orders for which *no* refund was issued. The solution involves adding a WHERE clause that tests for NULL values, as follows:

```
SELECT
Customers.FirstName AS 'First Name',
Customers.LastName AS 'Last Name',
Orders.OrderDate AS 'Order Date',
Orders.OrderAmount AS 'Order Amt'
FROM Customers
LEFT JOIN Orders
ON Customers.CustomerID = Orders.CustomerID
LEFT JOIN Refunds
ON Orders.OrderID = Refunds.OrderID
WHERE Orders.OrderID IS NOT NULL
AND Refunds.RefundID IS NULL
ORDER BY Customers.LastName, Customers.FirstName, Orders.OrderDate
```

The resulting data is:

First Name	Last Name	Order Date	Order Amt
Paul	Johnson	2016-09-15	20.00
Rumi	Shah	2016-09-02	12.50

The WHERE clause first tests Orders.OrderID to make sure that it isn't NULL. Doing so ensures that we don't see customers who never placed an order. The second line of the WHERE clause tests Refunds.RefundID to make sure that it is NULL. This guarantees that we only see orders that don't have a matching refund.

Notice that we didn't bother to display the Refund Date or Refund Amount columns in this SELECT. This is because we know those columns would always have NULL values, based on our selection criteria.

Right Joins

The previous SELECT statements utilized the LEFT JOIN keyword. The good news about right joins is that they are identical in concept to the left join. The only difference between left and right joins is the order in which the two tables in the join are listed.

In left joins, the primary table is listed to the left of the LEFT JOIN keyword. The secondary table, which may or may not contain matching rows, is listed to the right of the LEFT JOIN keyword.

In right joins, the primary table is listed to the right of the RIGHT JOIN keyword. The secondary table is listed to the left of the RIGHT JOIN keyword. That's the only difference.

The FROM clause and joins in the previous SELECT statement were:

```
FROM Customers
LEFT JOIN Orders
ON Customers.CustomerID = Orders.CustomerID
LEFT JOIN Refunds
ON Orders.OrderID = Refunds.OrderID
```

The equivalent logic, using RIGHT JOIN keywords is:

```
FROM Refunds
RIGHT JOIN Orders
ON Orders.OrderID = Refunds.OrderID
RIGHT JOIN Customers
ON Customers.CustomerID = Orders.CustomerID
```

Note that only the order in which tables are listed before and after the RIGHT JOIN matters. The order in which columns are listed after the ON keyword has no significance. Thus, the above is also equivalent to:

```
FROM Refunds
RIGHT JOIN Orders
ON Refunds.OrderID = Orders.OrderID
RIGHT JOIN Customers
ON Orders.CustomerID = Customers.CustomerID
```

In essence, if you're comfortable with the LEFT JOIN, it's completely unnecessary to ever use the RIGHT JOIN keyword. Anything that can be specified with a RIGHT JOIN can be stated as a LEFT JOIN. Our suggestion is therefore to stick with the LEFT JOIN, because it is usually more intuitive. Because we read from left to right, it's natural to think in terms of listing the more important, or primary, tables first.

Table Order in Outer Joins

We noted previously that the order in which tables are specified in an inner join is not significant. The same is *not* true of outer joins, because the order in which tables are listed in a left or right join is significant. At the same time, there is some flexibility in listing the tables in situations where there are three or more tables. The order of the LEFT (or RIGHT) JOIN keywords can be switched around if desired.

Let's look again at the original FROM clause and joins from the previous select:

```
FROM Customers
LEFT JOIN Orders
ON Customers.CustomerID = Orders.CustomerID
LEFT JOIN Refunds
ON Orders.OrderID = Refunds.OrderID
```

We've already seen that the Refunds table can be listed first and the Customers table last, as long as everything is converted to right joins, as in:

```
FROM Refunds
RIGHT JOIN Orders
ON Orders.OrderID = Refunds.OrderID
Right JOIN Customers
ON Customers.CustomerID = Orders.CustomerID
```

Is it possible to list the Customers table first, and then the Refunds table, followed by the Orders table? Yes, as long as you're willing to mix left and right joins together and also throw in some parentheses. The following is equivalent to the above:

```
FROM Customers
LEFT JOIN (Refunds
RIGHT JOIN Orders
ON Orders.OrderID = Refunds.OrderID)
ON Customers.CustomerID = Orders.CustomerID
```

What was a fairly simple statement has now turned into something unnecessarily complex. We only show this logic to indicate what *not* to do, and also because it's something that you may encounter when reviewing code. Our advice is to stick with the LEFT JOIN keyword and avoid parentheses when devising complex FROM clauses with multiple tables.

Full Joins

In addition to left joins and right joins, there is one additional outer join type, referred to as the *full join*. We've seen that in left and right joins, one table is primary and the other is secondary. Alternatively, you can say that one table is required and one is optional, which means that when matching two tables, rows in the secondary (or optional) table don't necessarily have to exist.

In the inner join, both tables are primary (or required). When matching two tables, there must be a match between both tables for a row of data to be selected.

In the full join, both tables are secondary (or optional). In this situation, if we're matching rows in Table A and Table B, then we display 1) all rows from Table A, even if there is no matching row in Table B, and also 2) all rows from Table B, even if there is no matching row in Table A.

Database Differences: MySQL

Unlike SQL Server and Oracle, MySQL doesn't allow for a full join.

Let's look at an example in which we are matching rows from these two tables. First, we have this Movies table:

MovieID	MovieTitle	Rating
1	Love Actually	R
2	North by Northwest	Not Rated
3	Love and Death	PG
4	The Truman Show	PG
5	Everyone Says I Love You	R
6	Down with Love	PG-13
7	Finding Nemo	G

Second, here's a Ratings table, with rating descriptions from the Motion Picture Association of America (MPAA):

RatingID	Rating	RatingDescription
1	G	General Audiences
2	PG	Parental Guidance Suggested
3	PG-13	Parents Strongly Cautioned
4	R	Restricted
5	NC-17	Under 17 Not Admitted

The Movies table has a list of movies in the database and includes the MPAA rating for each movie. The Ratings table has a list of the ratings and their descriptions. Let's say we want to find all matches between these two tables. We'll use a FULL JOIN to show all rows from the Movies table as well as all rows from the Ratings table. The full join will display all rows, even if a match from the other table isn't found. The SELECT looks like this:

```
SELECT
RatingDescription AS 'Rating Description',
MovieTitle AS 'Movie'
FROM Movies
FULL JOIN Ratings
ON Movies.Rating = Ratings.Rating
ORDER BY RatingDescription, MovieTitle
```

The output of this statement is:

Rating Description	Movie
NULL	North by Northwest
General Audiences	Finding Nemo
Parental Guidance Suggested	Love and Death
Parental Guidance Suggested	The Truman Show
Parents Strongly Cautioned	Down with Love
Restricted	Everyone Says I Love You
Under 17 Not Admitted	NULL

Notice that there are two NULL cells in the data, which is a direct result of having used a FULL JOIN. In the first instance, there is no rating shown for *North by Northwest* because there was no matching row in the Ratings table for that movie. In the second instance, there is no movie shown for the "Under 17 Not Admitted" rating description because there were no matching rows in the Movies table for that rating.

As a side note, observe that we chose not to use table aliases or specify table names in the *columnlist*. For example, we listed the column MovieTitle as is, without the fully qualified name (Movies.MovieTitle). This is because these columns exist only in one table, so there is no confusion in specifying a column name without the table name.

The FULL JOIN is seldom used in practice for the simple reason that this type of relationship between tables is relatively uncommon. In essence, the full join shows data where there are nonmatches in both directions between two tables. We are normally interested only in data where there is a complete match between two tables (the inner join) or perhaps a one-sided match (the left or right join).

Cross Joins

The final join type to be discussed in this chapter, the cross join, is neither an inner join nor an outer join. In essence, the cross join is a way of joining two tables without indicating any relationship between the tables. Because no relationship is stated, the cross join produces every combination of rows between the tables. In technical terms, this is referred to as the *Cartesian product*. If one table has three rows and a second table has four rows, and those tables are cross joined, the result will have 12 rows. Because of the esoteric nature of this join, it is seldom used in practice.

With that in mind, let's look at two examples of the cross join. In this first example, we'll imagine that we're a shirt maker, and we produce shirts in three sizes and in four colors. A SizeInventory table holds the available sizes and looks like this:

SizeID	Size
1	Small
2	Medium
3	Large

A ColorInventory table lists the available colors, and includes this data:

ColorID	Color
1	Red
2	Blue
3	Green
4	Yellow

We want to determine all of the possible combinations of shirt sizes and colors that can be produced. This can be accomplished by the following SELECT statement, using a cross join:

```
SELECT
Size,
Color
FROM SizeInventory
CROSS JOIN ColorInventory
```

The resulting output is:

Size	Color
Small	Red
Small	Blue
Small	Green
Small	Yellow
Medium	Red
Medium	Blue
Medium	Green
Medium	Yellow
Large	Red
Large	Blue
Large	Green
Large	Yellow

As you can see, the cross join produces every combination of rows from both tables. Notice that there is no ON keyword in a cross join. This is because no relationship between the tables is specified. The tables don't have a column in common. The data in both tables is independent of each other.

Interestingly, the cross join can also be specified in the "alternate" specification format discussed in the previous chapter. That is, the cross join can be indicated by merely listing both tables in the FROM clause, without the use of the CROSS JOIN keyword. The following SELECT is the equivalent of the previous CROSS JOIN statement and produces the same output:

```
SELECT
Size,
Color
FROM SizeInventory, ColorInventory
```

The preceding cross join example represents a situation that's not very realistic. However, this second example indicates a somewhat more common use of the cross join. For this example, we'll imagine that we have a special table with only one row of data that contains certain key pieces of information. Because that table has only one row of data, we can do a cross join to the table without increasing the number of rows in the final result. To illustrate, we'll use this SpecialDates table that contains a number of dates relevant to the organization:

LastProcessDate	CurrentFiscalYear	CurrentFiscalQuarter
2016-09-15	2016	Q3

In this scenario, we want to select data from our Orders table. However, we only want to see data for the LastProcessDate in the SpecialDates table. The LastProcessDate is a frequently changing date that gives the date of the last group of data processed in the system. The assumption is that there may be some sort of lag, so this may not be the current date. This statement, utilizing a cross join, accomplishes that objective.

```
SELECT
OrderID AS 'Order ID',
OrderDate AS 'Date',
OrderAmount AS 'Amount'
FROM Orders
CROSS JOIN SpecialDates
WHERE OrderDate = LastProcessDate
```

The resulting output is:

Order ID	Date	Amount
4	2016-09-15	20.00

Only one row of data from the Orders table is shown. This is because we've used the LastProcessDate of the SpecialDates table as part of the selection logic. Note that because the SpecialDates table has only one row, there is no harm in doing a cross join to this table. It doesn't affect the number of rows displayed.

Looking Ahead

This chapter extended our discussion of joins to outer joins. The left join enables the analyst to join a primary and secondary table together, showing all rows in the primary table even if there is no match in the secondary table. The right join is simply the reverse of the left join, switching the order of the primary and secondary tables. Finally, the full join enables both tables to be secondary tables. The full join displays all rows in either table, even if there is no match in the other table. We also talked about the cross join, a seldom used join type that shows all combinations of rows from both tables being joined. In a cross join, the relationship between the tables, if one exists, is not stated.

In our next chapter, "Self Joins and Views," we'll take another slight detour to two related topics. First, we'll discuss self joins, which is a special technique that allows us to join a table to itself. This creates a virtual view of the table, in the sense that we can now view this table from two different perspectives. The second main topic of the following chapter will extend the concept of self joins to a more general way of creating virtual views of multiple tables.

13

Self Joins and Views

Keywords Introduced

CREATE VIEW · ALTER VIEW · DROP VIEW

The inner and outer joins of the previous two chapters dealt with various ways of combining data from multiple tables. The assumption has always been that the data exists in physical tables in a database. We'll now turn to two techniques that will let us view data in a more virtual way. The first technique, the self join, allows the analyst to join a table to itself, referring to the same table twice, as if it were two separate tables. As such, the self join creates a virtual view of a table, allowing it to be used more than once. Second, we'll learn about database views, which is a useful concept that enables us to create new virtual tables at will.

Self Joins

The self join lets you join a table to itself. The most common use of the self join is in dealing with self-referencing tables. These are tables that include a column that refers to another column in the same table. A common example of this type of relationship is a table that contains information about employees.

In this next example, each row in a Personnel table has a column that points to another row in the same table, representing the employee's manager. In a way, this is similar to the concept of foreign keys. The main difference is that, whereas foreign keys point to a column in another table, we now have a situation where a column points to another column within the same table.

Let's look at the data in this Personnel table:

EmployeeID	EmployeeName	ManagerID
1	Susan Carter	NULL
2	Li Wang	1
3	Robert Baker	1
4	Scott Fielding	1
5	Carla Bender	2
6	Janet Brown	2
7	Jules Moreau	3
8	Amy Adamson	4
9	Jaideep Singh	4
10	Amelia Williams	5

This table has one row per employee. The ManagerID column states which manager the employee reports to. The ID number in that column corresponds to a value in the EmployeeID column. For example, Li Wang has a ManagerID of 1. This indicates that Li's manager is Susan Carter, who has an EmployeeID of 1.

We can see that the three people who report to Susan Carter are Li Wang, Robert Baker, and Scott Fielding. Notice that Susan Carter has no value in the ManagerID column. This indicates that she is the head of the company and thus has no manager.

Now, let's say that we want to list all employees and show the name of the manager to whom each employee reports. To accomplish this, we'll create a self-join of the Personnel table to itself. A table alias must always be used with self joins so that we have a way of distinguishing each instance of the table. We'll give the first instance of the Personnel table a table alias of Employees, and we'll give the second instance a table alias of Managers. Here's the statement:

```
SELECT
Employees.EmployeeName AS 'Employee Name',
Managers.EmployeeName AS 'Manager Name'
FROM Personnel AS Employees
INNER JOIN Personnel AS Managers
ON Employees.ManagerID = Managers.EmployeeID
ORDER BY Employees.EmployeeName
```

The resulting data is:

Employee Name	Manager Name
Amelia Williams	Carol Bender
Amy Adamson	Scott Fielding
Carla Bender	Li Wang
Jaideep Singh	Scott Fielding
Janet Brown	Li Wang
Jules Moreau	Robert Baker
Li Wang	Susan Carter
Robert Baker	Susan Carter
Scott Fielding	Susan Carter

The trickiest part of this SELECT is the ON clause in the join. To get the self join to work correctly, we must use the ON to establish a relationship between the ManagerID column of the Employees view of the Personnel table, and the EmployeeID column of the Managers view of the table. In other words, the indicated manager is also an employee.

Notice that Susan Carter isn't shown in the previous data as an employee. This is because we used an inner join in the statement. Because Susan Carter has no manager, there is no match to the Managers view of the table. If we want Susan Carter to be included, we merely need to change the inner join to an outer join. The new statement is:

```
SELECT
Employees.EmployeeName AS 'Employee Name',
Managers.EmployeeName AS 'Manager Name'
FROM Personnel AS Employees
LEFT JOIN Personnel AS Managers
ON Employees.ManagerID = Managers.EmployeeID
ORDER BY Employees.EmployeeName
```

The data retrieved is then:

Employee Name	Manager Name
Amelia Williams	Carol Bender
Amy Adamson	Scott Fielding
Carla Bender	Li Wang
Jaideep Singh	Scott Fielding
Janet Brown	Li Wang
Jules Moreau	Robert Baker
Li Wang	Susan Carter
Robert Baker	Susan Carter
Scott Fielding	Susan Carter
Susan Carter	NULL

Creating Views

The self join allows you to create multiple views of the same table. We'll now extend this concept, allowing us to create new views of any table or combination of tables.

Views are merely SELECT statements that have been saved in a database. Once saved, the view can be referred to as if it were a table in the database. Database tables contain physical data; views do not contain data but allow you to proceed as if a view were a real table with data. Views can therefore be thought of as virtual tables. Additionally, views are permanent, not temporary. Once created, a view continues to be referenced until the view itself is deleted.

You might ask why views are necessary. We'll get into the benefits of views later in the chapter, but in short, views provide added flexibility as to how data can be accessed. Whether a database has been around for a few days or for years, the data in that database is stored in tables in a very specific manner. As time progresses, requirements for accessing that data change, but it isn't a trivial matter to reorganize the tables to meet new requirements. The great advantage of views is that they allow the analyst to create new virtual views of the data already in a database. Views allow you to create the equivalent of new tables without having to physically rearrange data. As such, views add a dynamic element to a database design by keeping it fresh and up to date.

How is a view stored in a database? All relational databases consist of a number of different object types. The most important object type is the table. However, most database management software allows users to save any number of other object types. The most common of these are views and stored procedures. There are often many other object types in a database, such as functions and triggers.

SQL provides the CREATE VIEW keyword to enable users to create new views. The general syntax is as follows:

```
CREATE VIEW ViewName AS
SelectStatement
```

After the view is created, the *ViewName* is used to reference the data that would be returned from the *SelectStatement* in the view. Here's an example. In the previous chapter, we looked at this SELECT statement:

```
SELECT
Customers.FirstName AS 'First Name',
Customers.LastName AS 'Last Name',
Orders.OrderDate AS 'Order Date',
Orders.OrderAmount AS 'Order Amt',
Refunds.RefundDate AS 'Refund Date',
Refunds.RefundAmount AS 'Refund Amt'
FROM Customers
LEFT JOIN Orders
ON Customers.CustomerID = Orders.CustomerID
LEFT JOIN Refunds
ON Orders.OrderID = Refunds.OrderID
ORDER BY Customers.LastName, Customers.FirstName, Orders.OrderDate
```

This statement returned this data:

First Name	Last Name	Order Date	Order Amt	Refund Date	Refund Amt
Sara	Davis	2016-09-01	10.00	2016-09-02	5.00
Paul	Johnson	2016-09-15	20.00	NULL	NULL
Samuel	Martinez	NULL	NULL	NULL	NULL
Rumi	Shah	2016-09-02	12.50	NULL	NULL
Rumi	Shah	2016-09-03	18.00	2015-09-18	18.00

To set up this SELECT statement as a view, we simply place the entire SELECT in a CREATE VIEW statement, as follows:

```
CREATE VIEW CustomersOrdersRefunds AS
SELECT
Customers.FirstName AS 'First Name',
Customers.LastName AS 'Last Name',
Orders.OrderDate AS 'Order Date',
Orders.OrderAmount AS 'Order Amt',
Refunds.RefundDate AS 'Refund Date',
Refunds.RefundAmount AS 'Refund Amt'
FROM Customers
LEFT JOIN Orders
ON Customers.CustomerID = Orders.CustomerID
LEFT JOIN Refunds
ON Orders.OrderID = Refunds.OrderID
```

The only item missing in the above CREATE VIEW is the ORDER BY clause of the original SELECT statement. Because views aren't stored as physical data, there is never a reason to include an ORDER BY clause for a view.

Referencing Views

When we execute the above CREATE VIEW statement, it creates a view called CustomersOrdersRefunds. Creating the view does not return any data. It merely defines the view for later use. To use the view to bring back data as before, you would execute this SELECT statement:

```
SELECT *
FROM CustomersOrdersRefunds
```

This retrieves:

First Name	Last Name	Order Date	Order Amt	Refund Date	Refund Amt
Sara	Davis	2016-09-01	10.00	2016-09-02	5.00
Rumi	Shah	2016-09-02	12.50	NULL	NULL
Rumi	Shah	2016-09-03	18.00	2015-09-18	18.00
Paul	Johnson	2016-09-15	20.00	NULL	NULL
Samuel	Martinez	NULL	NULL	NULL	NULL

Notice that this data is displayed in a different row order than what was originally retrieved. This is because the view does not contain an ORDER BY clause. As a result, the data is returned in the order in which it is physically stored in the database. This is easily corrected by adding an ORDER BY clause to the SELECT, as follows:

```
SELECT *
FROM CustomersOrdersRefunds
ORDER BY [Last Name], [First Name], [Order Date]
```

This now returns the data in the expected order. Remember that columns in views must be referenced by the column aliases specified when the view was created. We can no longer reference the original column names. In this example, the CustomersOrdersRefunds view applied a column alias of "Last Name" to the LastName column in the Customers table. We therefore need to reference the column alias in the ORDER BY clause. As mentioned in Chapter 2, we need to include brackets around each of these column names in the ORDER BY clause to allow for correct interpretation of the embedded spaces.

Database Differences: MySQL and Oracle

MySQL and Oracle use different characters around columns containing spaces. MySQL uses the accent grave (`). Oracle uses double quotes (").

Once a view is created, it can be referenced and utilized just like any other table. For example, we might want to see only a few selected columns from the view and select only one specific customer. To do that, we can issue a SELECT statement such as:

```
SELECT
[First Name],
[Last Name],
[Order Date]
FROM CustomersOrdersRefunds
WHERE [Last Name] = 'Shah'
```

The output is:

First Name	Last Name	Order Date
Rumi	Shajh	2016-09-02
Rumi	Shah	2016-09-03

As before, we need to place square brackets around each of the column names because they contain embedded spaces.

Benefits of Views

The previous example illustrates one of the important benefits of using views. Once a view is created, that view can be referenced just as if it were a table. Even if the view references multiple tables joined together, it now appears, logically, to be just one table.

Let's summarize the benefits of using views:

- **Views can reduce complexity.** First, views can simplify SELECT statements that are particularly complex. For example, if you have a SELECT statement that joins six tables together, it might be useful to create views with two or three tables each. You can then reference those views in a SELECT statement that is less complex than the original.

- **Views can increase reusability.** In a situation where three tables are always joined together, you can create a view with those three tables. Then, instead of always having to join those three tables every time you query data, you can simply reference a predefined view.

- **Views can properly format data.** If columns are incorrectly formatted in the database, you can use the CAST or other functions to format that column exactly as desired. For example, you might have a date column stored as an integer datatype in the database, in a YYYYMMDD format. It might be advantageous to view this data as a date/time column so it can be presented and manipulated as a true date. To accomplish this, you can create a view on the table that transforms the column to the proper format. All subsequent references to that table can then reference the new view rather than the table.

- **Views can create calculated columns.** Suppose two columns in a table include Quantity and PricePerItem. End users are usually interested in the total price, which is calculated by multiplying the two columns together. You can create a view of the original table with a new calculated column with this calculation. Users can then reference the view and always have the calculation available.

- **Views can be used to rename column names.** If a database contains cryptic column names, you can create views with column aliases to translate those names into something more meaningful.

- **Views can create a subset of data.** Let's say a database contains a table with all of your customers. Most of your users need only to see customers who have placed an order during the prior year. You can easily create a view of this table that includes this useful subset of data.

- **Views can be used to enforce security restrictions.** Often you want certain users to be able to access only certain columns in a given table. To accomplish this, you can create a view of the table for those users. The security features of the database can then be used to grant access to the new view for those users, while restricting them from accessing the underlying table.

Modifying and Deleting Views

After a view is created, it can be easily modified using the ALTER VIEW statement. Here's the general syntax:

```
ALTER VIEW ViewName AS
SelectStatement
```

When altering a view, you must specify the entire SELECT statement contained in the view. The original SELECT in the view gets replaced by the new SELECT. Let's say we originally created a view with this statement:

```
CREATE VIEW CustomersView AS
SELECT
FirstName AS 'First Name',
LastName as 'Last Name'
FROM Customers
```

To add a new column to this view for a CustomerID, we would issue a statement such as:

```
ALTER VIEW CustomersView AS
SELECT
FirstName AS 'First Name',
LastName AS 'Last Name',
CustomerID AS 'Cust ID'
FROM Customers
```

Once again, creating or altering a view does not return any data. It merely creates or modifies the definition of the view.

Database Differences: Oracle

Unlike SQL Server and MySQL, the ALTER VIEW command in Oracle is more restrictive. To accomplish the previous ALTER VIEW in Oracle, you need to issue a DROP VIEW and then a CREATE VIEW with the new definition.

The DROP VIEW statement is used to delete a previously created view. The syntax is:

```
DROP VIEW ViewName
```

To delete the CustomersView created earlier, we can issue this statement:

```
DROP VIEW CustomersView
```

Looking Ahead

Self joins and views are two different ways of viewing data in a virtual manner. The self join allows the analyst to join a table to itself. Self joins are useful with self-referential data, where one column in a table can be joined to another column in the same table.

Database views are much more flexible. Essentially, any SELECT statement can be saved as a view, which can then be referenced as if it were a physical table. Unlike tables, views do not contain any data. They merely define a new virtual view of data in existing tables. As such, views serve a wide variety of functions, from reducing complexity to reformatting data. Once created, views can be modified or deleted with the ALTER VIEW and DELETE VIEW statements.

In our next chapter, "Subqueries," we'll return to a topic more directly related to our previous discussion of how to join tables together. Subqueries provide a method of relating tables to each other without making explicit use of an inner or outer join. Because of the wide variety of ways that subqueries can be structured and used, this is probably the most difficult subject in this book. However, an understanding of subqueries can be tremendously rewarding. There's actually quite a bit of flexibility in how subqueries can be used. As such, this lends itself to a certain amount of creativity in your query designs.

14

Subqueries

Keywords Introduced

EXISTS · WITH

In Chapter 4, we talked about composite functions: functions that contained other functions. Similarly, SQL queries can contain other queries. Queries contained within other queries are called *subqueries*.

The topic of subqueries is somewhat complex, primarily because there are many different ways in which they can be used. Subqueries can be found in many different parts of the SELECT statement, each with different nuances and requirements. As a query contained within another query, a subquery can be related to and dependent on the main query, or it can be completely independent of the main query. Again, this distinction results in different requirements for their usage.

No matter how subqueries are used, they add a great deal of flexibility to the ways in which you can write SQL queries. Often, subqueries provide functionality that could be accomplished by other means. In such instances, personal preference will come into play as you decide whether or not to utilize the subquery solution. However, as you'll see, in certain situations subqueries are absolutely essential for the task at hand.

With that said, let's begin our discussion with an outline of the basic types of subqueries.

Types of Subqueries

Subqueries can be used not only with SELECT statements but also with the INSERT, UPDATE, and DELETE statements that will be covered in Chapter 17, "Modifying Data." In this chapter, however, we'll restrict our discussion of subqueries to the SELECT statement.

Here's the general SELECT statement we've seen previously:

```
SELECT columnlist
FROM tablelist
WHERE condition
GROUP BY columnlist
HAVING condition
ORDER BY columnlist
```

Subqueries can be inserted into virtually any of the clauses in the SELECT statement. However, the way in which the subquery is stated and used varies slightly, depending on whether it is used in a *columnlist*, *tablelist*, or *condition*.

But what exactly is a subquery? A subquery is merely a SELECT statement that has been inserted inside another SQL statement. The results returned from the subquery are used within the context of the overall SQL query. Additionally, there can be more than one subquery in a SQL statement. To summarize, subqueries can be specified in three main ways:

- When a subquery is part of a *tablelist*, it specifies a data source. This applies to situations where the subquery is part of a FROM clause.
- When a subquery is part of a *condition*, it becomes part of the selection criteria. This applies to situations where the subquery is part of a WHERE or HAVING clause.
- When a subquery is part of a *columnlist*, it creates a single calculated column. This applies to situations where the subquery is part of a SELECT, GROUP BY, or ORDER BY clause.

The remainder of this chapter explains each of these three scenarios in detail.

Using a Subquery as a Data Source

When a subquery is specified as part of the FROM clause, it instantly creates a new data source. This is similar to the concept of creating a view and then referencing that view in a SELECT. The only difference is that a view is permanently saved in a database. A subquery used as a data source isn't saved. It exists only temporarily, as part of the SELECT statement. Nevertheless, you can think of a subquery in a FROM clause as a type of virtual view.

Let's first consider an example that illustrates how subqueries can be used as a data source. Let's say we have this Users table:

UserID	UserName
1	Cecilia Rodriguez
2	Elaine Bundy
3	Rakesh Gupta
4	April Waters

We also have this Transactions table:

TransactionID	UserID	TransactionAmount	TransactionType
1	1	22.25	Cash
2	2	11.75	Credit
3	2	5.00	Credit
4	2	8.00	Cash
5	3	9.33	Credit
6	3	10.11	Credit

This data is actually quite similar to the Customers and Orders tables we've seen in previous chapters. The Users table resembles the Customers table, except that we've combined the first and last names into a single column. The Transactions table has entries similar to orders, except that we've added a TransactionType column, indicating whether the transaction was cash or credit. We've also dispensed with the date column that would normally be present.

We would like to see a list of users, along with a total sum of the cash transactions they have placed. The following SELECT accomplishes that task:

```
SELECT
UserName AS 'User Name',
ISNULL(CashTransactions.TotalCash, 0) AS 'Total Cash'
FROM Users
LEFT JOIN

(SELECT
UserID,
SUM(TransactionAmount) AS 'TotalCash'
FROM Transactions
WHERE TransactionType = 'Cash'
GROUP BY UserID) AS CashTransactions

ON Users.UserID = CashTransactions.UserID
ORDER BY Users.UserID
```

Two blank lines were inserted to clearly separate the subquery from the rest of the statement. The subquery is the middle section of the statement. The results are:

User Name	Total Cash
Cecilia Rodriguez	22.25
Elaine Bundy	8.00
Rakesh Gupta	0
April Waters	0

April Waters shows no cash transactions, because she made no transactions at all. Although Rakesh Gupta has two transactions, they were both credit transactions, so he also shows no cash. Note that the ISNULL function converts the NULL values that would normally appear for Rakesh and April to a 0.

Let's now analyze how the subquery works. The subquery in the previous statement is:

```
SELECT
UserID,
SUM(TransactionAmount) AS 'TotalCash'
FROM Transactions
WHERE TransactionType = 'Cash'
GROUP BY UserID
```

In general form, the main SELECT statement in the above is:

```
SELECT
UserName AS 'User Name'
ISNULL(CashTransactions.TotalCash, 0) AS 'Total Cash'
FROM Users
LEFT JOIN (subquery) AS CashTransactions
ON Users.UserID = CashTransactions.UserID
ORDER BY Users.UserID
```

If the subquery were executed on its own, the results would be:

UserID	TotalCash
1	22.25
2	8.00

We see data for only users 1 and 2. The WHERE clause in the subquery enforces the requirement that we look only at cash orders.

The entire subquery is then referenced as if it were a separate table or view. Notice that the subquery is given a table alias of CashTransactions. This allows the columns in the subquery to be referenced in the main SELECT. As such, the following line in the main SELECT references data in the subquery:

```
ISNULL(CashTransactions.TotalCash, 0) AS 'Total Cash'
```

CashTransactions.TotalCash is a column taken from the subquery.

You might ask whether it was truly necessary to use a subquery to obtain the desired data. In this case, the answer is yes. We might have attempted to simply join the Users and Transactions tables via a LEFT JOIN, as in the following:

```
SELECT
UserName AS 'User Name',
SUM(TransactionAmount) AS 'Total Cash Transactions'
FROM Users
LEFT JOIN Transactions
ON Users.UserID = Transactions.UserID
WHERE TransactionType = 'Cash'
GROUP BY Users.UserID, Users.UserName
ORDER BY Users.UserID
```

However, this statement yields the following data:

User Name	Total Cash
Cecilia Rodriguez	22.25
Elaine Bundy	8.00

We no longer see any rows for Rakesh Gupta or April Waters, because the WHERE clause exclusion for cash orders is now in the main query rather than in a subquery. As a result, we don't see any data for people who didn't place cash orders.

Using a Subquery in Selection Criteria

In Chapter 7, we introduced the first format of the IN operator. The example we used was:

```
WHERE State IN ('IL', 'NY')
```

In this format, the IN operator merely lists a number of values in parentheses. There is also a second format for the IN, in which an entire SELECT statement is inserted inside the parentheses. For example, a list of states might be specified as:

```
WHERE State IN
(SELECT
States
FROM StateTable
WHERE Region = 'Midwest')
```

Rather than list individual states, this second format allows us to generate a dynamic list of states through more complex logic.

Let's illustrate with an example that uses the Users and Transactions tables. In this scenario, we want to retrieve a list of users who have ever paid cash for any transaction. A SELECT that accomplishes this is:

```
SELECT UserName AS 'User Name'
FROM Users
WHERE UserID IN
(SELECT UserID
FROM Transactions
WHERE TransactionType = 'Cash')
```

The resulting data is:

User Name
Cecilia Rodriguez
Elaine Bundy

Rakesh Gupta is not included in the list because, although he has transactions, none of them were in cash. Notice that the subquery SELECT is placed entirely within the parentheses for the IN keyword. There is only one column, UserID, in the *columnlist* of the subquery. This is a requirement, because we want the subquery to produce the equivalent of a list of values for only one column. Also note that the UserID column is used to connect the two queries. Although we're displaying UserName, we're using UserID to define the relationship between the Users and Transactions tables.

Once again, we can ask whether it's necessary to use a subquery, and this time the answer is no. Here is an equivalent query that returns the same data.

```
SELECT UserName AS 'User Name'
FROM Users
INNER JOIN Transactions
ON Users.UserID = Transactions.UserID
WHERE TransactionType = 'Cash'
GROUP BY Users.UserName
```

Without using a subquery, we can directly join the Users and Transactions tables. However, a GROUP BY clause is now needed to ensure that we bring back only one row per user.

Correlated Subqueries

The subqueries we've seen so far have been uncorrelated subqueries. Generally speaking, all subqueries can be classified as either *uncorrelated* or *correlated*. These terms describe whether the subquery is related to the query in which it is contained. Uncorrelated subqueries are unrelated. When a subquery is unrelated, that means it is completely independent of the outer query. Uncorrelated subqueries are evaluated and executed only once as part of the entire SELECT statement. Furthermore, uncorrelated subqueries can stand on their own. If you wanted to, you could execute an uncorrelated subquery as a separate query.

In contrast, correlated subqueries are specifically related to the outer query. Because of this explicit relationship, correlated subqueries must be evaluated for each row returned and can produce different results each time the subquery is executed. Correlated subqueries can't be executed on their own, because some element in the query makes it dependent on the outer query.

The best way to explain is with an example. Returning to the Users and Transactions tables, let's say we want to produce a list of users who have a total transaction amount less than 20 dollars. Here's a statement that accomplishes that request:

```
SELECT
UserName AS 'User Name'
FROM Users
WHERE
(SELECT
SUM(TransactionAmount)
FROM Transactions
WHERE Users.UserID = Transactions.UserID)
< 20
```

The result is:

User Name
Rakesh Gupta

What makes this subquery correlated, as opposed to uncorrelated? The answer can be seen by looking at the subquery itself:

```
SELECT
SUM(TransactionAmount)
FROM Transactions
WHERE Users.UserID = Transactions.UserID
```

This subquery is correlated because it cannot be executed on its own. If run by itself, this subquery would produce an error because the Users.UserID column in the WHERE clause doesn't exist within the context of the subquery. To understand what's going on, it's helpful to look at the entire SELECT statement in a more general way:

```
SELECT
UserName AS 'User Name'
FROM Users
WHERE
SubqueryResult < 20
```

The subquery returns a *columnlist* with a single value, which we're calling *SubqueryResult*. As a correlated subquery, the subquery must be evaluated for each user. Also, note that this type of subquery demands that it only returns a single row and a single value. The *SubqueryResult* couldn't be evaluated if there were more than one row or value involved.

As before, you might ask whether a subquery is necessary, and once again the answer is no. Here's an equivalent statement that produces the same result:

```
SELECT
UserName AS 'User Name'
FROM Users
LEFT JOIN Transactions
ON Users.UserID = Transactions.UserID
GROUP BY Users.UserID, Users.UserName
HAVING SUM(TransactionAmount) < 20
```

Notice, however, that without a subquery, the equivalent statement now requires GROUP BY and HAVING clauses. The GROUP BY clause creates groups of users, and the HAVING clause enforces the requirement that each group must have transacted less than 20 dollars.

The EXISTS Operator

An additional technique associated with correlated subqueries uses a special operator called EXISTS. This operator allows you to determine whether data in a correlated subquery exists. Let's say that we want to discover which users have made any transactions. This can be accomplished with the use of the EXISTS operator in this statement:

```
SELECT
UserName AS 'User Name'
FROM Users
WHERE EXISTS
(SELECT *
FROM Transactions
WHERE Users.UserID = Transactions.UserID)
```

This statement returns:

User Name
Cecilia Rodriguez
Elaine Bundy
Rakesh Gupta

This is a correlated subquery because it cannot be executed on its own without reference to the main query. The EXISTS keyword in the above statement is evaluated as true if the SELECT in the correlated subquery returns any data. Notice that the subquery selects all columns (SELECT *). Because it doesn't matter which particular columns are selected in the subquery, we use the asterisk to return all columns. We're interested only in determining whether any data exists in the subquery. The result is that the query returns all users except April Waters. She doesn't appear because she has made no transactions.

As before, the logic in this statement can be expressed in other ways. Here's a statement that obtains the same results by using a subquery with the IN operator:

```
SELECT
UserName AS 'User Name'
FROM Users
WHERE UserID IN
(SELECT UserID
FROM Transactions)
```

This statement is probably easier to comprehend.

Here's yet another statement that retrieves the same data without the use of a subquery:

```
SELECT
UserName AS 'User Name'
FROM Users
INNER JOIN Transactions
ON Users.UserID = Transactions.UserID
GROUP BY UserName
```

In this statement, the INNER JOIN enforces the requirement that the user must also exist in the Transactions table. Also note that this query requires the use of a GROUP BY clause to avoid returning more than one row per user.

Using a Subquery as a Calculated Column

The final general use of subqueries is as a calculated column. Suppose we would like to see a list of users, along with a count of the number of transactions they have placed. This can be accomplished without subqueries using this statement:

```
SELECT
UserName AS 'User Name',
COUNT(TransactionID) AS 'Number of Transactions'
FROM Users
LEFT JOIN Transactions
ON Users.UserID = Transactions.UserID
GROUP BY Users.UserID, Users.UserName
ORDER BY Users.UserID
```

The output is:

User Name	Number of Transactions
Cecilia Rodriguez	1
Elaine Bundy	3
Rakesh Gupta	2
April Waters	0

Notice that we used a LEFT JOIN to accommodate users who may not have made any transactions. The GROUP BY enforces the requirement that we end up with one row per user. The COUNT function produces a count of the number of rows in the Transactions table.

Another way of obtaining the same result is to use a subquery as a calculated column. This looks like the following:

```
SELECT
UserName AS 'User Name',
(SELECT
COUNT(TransactionID)
FROM Transactions
WHERE Users.UserID = Transactions.UserID)
AS 'Number of Transactions'
FROM Users
ORDER BY Users.UserID
```

In this example, the subquery is a correlated subquery. The subquery cannot be executed on its own, because it references a column from the Users table in the WHERE clause. This subquery returns a calculated column for the SELECT *columnlist*. In other words, after the subquery is evaluated, it returns a single value, which is then included in the *columnlist*. Here's the general format of the previous statement:

```
SELECT
UserName AS 'User Name',
SubqueryResult AS 'Number of Transactions'
FROM Users
ORDER BY Users.UserID
```

As seen, the entire subquery returns a single value, which is used for the Number of Transactions column.

Common Table Expressions

An alternate subquery syntax allows it to be defined explicitly prior to the execution of the main query. This is known as a *common table expression*. In this syntax, the entire subquery is removed from its normal location and stated at the top of the query. The WITH keyword is used to indicate the presence of a common table expression. Although they may be used with correlated subqueries, a common table expression is far more useful for uncorrelated subqueries. To illustrate, let's return to the first subquery presented in this chapter:

```
SELECT
UserName AS 'User Name',
ISNULL(CashTransactions.TotalCash, 0) AS 'Total Cash'
FROM Users
LEFT JOIN

(SELECT
UserID,
SUM(TransactionAmount) AS 'TotalCash'
FROM Transactions
WHERE TransactionType = 'Cash'
GROUP BY UserID) AS CashTransactions

ON Users.UserID = CashTransactions.UserID
ORDER BY Users.UserID
```

As seen, the subquery in the above statement is given an alias of CashTransactions, and is joined to the Users table on the UserID column. The purpose of the subquery is to provide a total of the cash transactions for each user. The output of this query is:

User Name	Total Cash
Cecilia Rodriguez	22.25
Elaine Bundy	8.00
Rakesh Gupta	0
April Waters	0

We'll now present an alternate way of expressing this same logic, using a common table expression. The query looks like this:

```
WITH CashTransactions AS
(SELECT
UserID,
SUM(TransactionAmount) as TotalCash
FROM Transactions
WHERE TransactionType = 'Cash'
GROUP BY UserID)

SELECT
UserName AS 'User Name',
ISNULL(CashTransactions.TotalCash, 0) AS 'Total Cash'
FROM Users
LEFT JOIN CashTransactions
ON Users.UserID = CashTransactions.UserID
ORDER BY Users.UserID
```

In this alternative expression, the entire subquery has been moved to the top, prior to the main SELECT query. The WITH keyword indicates that a common table expression follows. The first line indicates that CashTransactions is an alias for the common table expression. The common table expression follows the AS keyword and is enclosed within parentheses.

We've inserted a blank line to separate the common table expression from the primary query. The following line in the main query:

```
LEFT JOIN CashTransactions
```

initiates the outer join to the common table expression, which is referenced via the CashTransactions alias. The chief virtue of the common table expression is its simplicity. The main query becomes easier to comprehend, because the details of the subquery now appear as a separate entity before the main query. The output of this query with a common table expression is identical to the original query with a subquery.

In short, it's really a matter of personal preference as to whether you'd like to use common table expressions in your queries. Whereas subqueries are embedded in a larger query, common table expressions state the subqueries up front.

Database Differences: MySQL

Unlike SQL Server and Oracle, MySQL doesn't support common table expressions.

Looking Ahead

In this chapter, we've seen subqueries used in three different ways: as a data source, in selection criteria, and as a calculated column. Additionally, we've seen examples of both correlated and uncorrelated subqueries. Finally, we briefly demonstrated the use of an alternate method of expressing subqueries using the common table expression. As such, we've really only touched on some of the uses of subqueries. What complicates the matter is that many subqueries can be expressed in other ways. Whether or not you choose to use subqueries depends on your personal taste and sometimes on the performance of the statement.

Through our use of joins and subqueries, we've explored numerous ways to select data from multiple tables. In our next chapter, "Set Logic," we'll look at a method of combining entire queries into a single SQL statement. This is a special type of logic that allows us to merge multiple data sets into a single result. As you'll see, set logic procedures are sometimes necessary in order to display sets of data that are only partially related to each other. As with subqueries, the techniques of set logic provide additional flexibility and logical possibilities for your SQL statements.

15

Set Logic

Keywords Introduced

UNION · UNION ALL · INTERSECT · EXCEPT

The various joins and subqueries of the previous few chapters have dealt with different ways of combining data from multiple tables. The result, however, has always been a single SELECT statement. Now we'll extend the concept of combining data in multiple tables to the possibility of combining data from multiple queries. In other words, we'll look at a way to write a single SQL statement that contains more than one SELECT to retrieve data.

The concept of combining queries is often referred to as *set logic*, a term taken from mathematics. Each SELECT query can be referred to as a *set* of data. The set logic we'll employ and examine in this chapter will address four basic scenarios. Assuming that we have data in SET A and in SET B, here are the four possibilities for retrieving data from the two sets:

- Data that is in SET A or in SET B
- Data that is in both SET A and SET B
- Data that is in SET A but not in SET B
- Data that is in SET B but not in SET A

We'll start by looking at the first scenario, for which we want data included in SET A or in SET B. As we'll see, this is the most prevalent and important of the set logic possibilities.

Using the UNION Operator

The UNION operator in SQL is used to handle logic to select data in either SET A or SET B. This is by far the most common situation. We'll start with an example. Let's say we have two tables in our database. The first is an Orders table containing data on orders placed by customers. We'll use the same Orders table seen in the previous few chapters:

OrderID	CustomerID	OrderDate	OrderAmount
1	1	2016-09-01	10.00
2	2	2016-09-02	12.50
3	2	2016-09-03	18.00
4	3	2016-09-15	20.00

The second table, named Returns, contains data on merchandise returned by customers. It might look like this:

ReturnID	CustomerID	ReturnDate	ReturnAmount
1	1	2016-09-10	2.00
2	2	2016-09-15	15.00
3	3	2016-09-28	3.00

Note that, unlike the Refunds table seen in Chapters 12 and 13, this Returns table is not directly related to the Orders table. In other words, returns are not tied to a specific order. In this scenario, a customer might return merchandise from multiple orders in a single refund transaction.

We want to create a report of all orders and returns from one particular customer. We would like the results sorted either by the order date if it's an order, or the return date if it's a return. Following is a statement that can accomplish this. We've inserted a few extra blank lines in this statement to emphasize the fact that it contains two completely separate SELECTs, combined by the UNION operator:

```
SELECT
OrderDate AS 'Date',
'Order' AS 'Type',
OrderAmount AS 'Amount'
FROM Orders
WHERE CustomerID = 2

UNION

SELECT
ReturnDate as 'Date',
'Return' AS 'Type',
ReturnAmount AS 'Amount'
FROM Returns
WHERE CustomerID = 2

ORDER BY Date
```

The resulting data is:

Date	Type	Amount
2016-09-02	Order	12.50
2016-09-03	Order	18.00
2016-09-15	Return	15.00

As you can see, the UNION operator separates two SELECT statements. Each of these SELECT statements would be capable of being run on its own. There is also an ORDER BY clause at the very end, which applies to the results of both SELECT statements. The general format for the previous statement is:

```
SelectStatementOne
UNION
SelectStatementTwo
ORDER BY columnlist
```

In order for the UNION to work, three rules must be followed:

- All SELECT statements combined with a UNION must have the same number of columns in the SELECT *columnlist*.
- All columns in each SELECT *columnlist* must be in the same order.
- All corresponding columns in each SELECT columnlist must have the same, or compatible, datatypes.

With reference to these rules, notice that both SELECT statements in the query have three columns. Each of the three columns has data in the same order and with the same datatype.

When using the UNION, you should use column aliases to give the same column name to all corresponding columns. In our example, the first column of the first SELECT has an original name of OrderDate. The first column of the second SELECT has an original name of ReturnDate. To ensure that the first column in the final result has the desired name, both OrderDate and ReturnDate are given a column alias of Date. This also allows the column to be referenced in an ORDER BY *columnlist*.

Also notice that the second column of each SELECT uses literal values. We created a calculated column named Type, which has a value of either Order or Return. This allows us to determine which table each row comes from.

Finally, notice that the ORDER BY clause applies to the final results of both queries combined. This is how it should be, because there would be no point in applying a sort to the individual queries.

At this point, it's useful to step back and talk about why it was necessary to employ the UNION operator rather than simply joining the Orders and Returns tables together in a single SELECT statement. Because both tables have a CustomerID column, why didn't we join the two tables together on this column? The problem with that approach is that the two tables are really only indirectly related to each other. Customers can place orders and customers can initiate returns, but there is no direct connection between orders and returns.

Additionally, even if there were a direct connection between the two tables, a join would not accomplish what is desired. With a proper join, related information can be placed together on the same row. In this case, however, we are interested in showing orders and returns on separate rows. The UNION operator must be used to display data in this manner.

In essence, the UNION allows us to retrieve unrelated or partially related data in a single statement.

Distinct and Non-Distinct Unions

There are actually two variations of the UNION operator: UNION and UNION ALL. There is only a slight difference between the two. The UNION operator eliminates all duplicate rows. The UNION ALL operator specifies that all rows will be included, even if they are duplicates.

The UNION operator eliminates duplicates in a manner similar to the DISTINCT keyword seen previously. Whereas DISTINCT applies to a single SELECT, the UNION eliminates duplicates in all SELECT statements combined via the UNION.

In the previous example with the Orders and Returns tables, there was no possibility of duplication, so it didn't matter which variation of the UNION was used. Here's an example that illustrates the difference. Let's say that we were only interested in the dates on which any order or return was issued. We don't want to see multiple rows for the same date. The following statement accomplishes this task.

```
SELECT
OrderDate AS 'Date'
FROM Orders
UNION
SELECT
ReturnDate as 'Date'
FROM Returns
ORDER BY Date
```

The resulting data is:

Date
2016-09-01
2016-09-02
2016-09-03
2016-09-10
2016-09-15
2016-09-28

Notice that there is only one row with the date 2016-09-15. Even though there is one row with 2016-09-15 in the Orders table and one row with 2016-09-15 in the Returns table, the UNION operator ensures that the 2016-09-15 date is listed only once.

If for some reason we wanted to see the date 2016-09-15 listed twice, we could employ the UNION ALL operator to accomplish this:

```
SELECT
OrderDate AS 'Date'
FROM Orders
UNION ALL
SELECT
ReturnDate as 'Date'
FROM Returns
ORDER BY Date
```

The output is now:

Date
2016-09-01
2016-09-02
2016-09-03
2016-09-10
2016-09-15
2016-09-15
2016-09-28

As you can see, the UNION ALL operator allows duplicate rows to be displayed.

Intersecting Queries

The UNION and UNION ALL operators return data in either of the sets specified in the two SELECT statements being combined. This is like using an OR operator to combine data from two logical sets.

SQL provides an operator called INTERSECT that only pulls data that is in both of the two sets being looked at. The INTERSECT is analogous to the AND operator and handles the second scenario stated at the beginning of this chapter:

- Data that is in both SET A and SET B

Database Differences: MySQL

MySQL doesn't support the INTERSECT operator.

Using the same Orders and Returns tables, suppose we want to see dates on which there are both orders and returns. A statement that accomplishes this is:

```
SELECT
OrderDate AS 'Date'
FROM Orders
INTERSECT
SELECT
ReturnDate as 'Date'
FROM Returns
ORDER BY Date
```

The result is:

Date
2016-09-15

Only one row is shown because this is the only date that appears in both the Orders and Returns tables.

There is one additional variation on the INTERSECT operator, which is provided by the EXCEPT operator. Whereas the INTERSECT returns data that is in both sets, the EXCEPT returns data that is in one set but not the other. Accordingly, this handles the third and fourth scenarios stated at the beginning of this chapter:

- Data that is in SET A but not in SET B
- Data that is in SET B but not in SET A

The general format of the EXCEPT is:

```
SelectStatementOne
EXCEPT
SelectStatementTwo
ORDER BY columnlist
```

This statement will show data that is in *SelectStatementOne* but not in *SelectStatementTwo*. Here's an example:

```
SELECT
OrderDate AS 'Date'
FROM Orders
EXCEPT
SELECT
ReturnDate as 'Date'
FROM Returns
ORDER BY Date
```

The result is:

Date
2016-09-01
2016-09-02
2016-09-03

This data shows dates on which orders were placed where no refunds were issued on that same date. Notice that 2016-09-15 does not appear, because a refund was issued on that date.

> **Database Differences: MySQL and Oracle**
>
> MySQL doesn't support the EXCEPT operator.
>
> The equivalent of the EXCEPT operator in Oracle is MINUS.

Looking Ahead

This chapter illustrated a variety of ways to use set logic to combine multiple sets of SELECT statements into a single statement. The most commonly used operator is the UNION, which allows you to combine data that is in either of two different sets. As such, the UNION is analogous to the OR operator. The UNION ALL is a variant of the UNION that allows duplicate rows to be shown. Similarly, the INTERCEPT operator allows data to be presented if it is in both of the sets of data being combined. The INTERCEPT is analogous to the AND operator. Finally, the EXCEPT operator allows for selection of data that is in one set but not in another.

Our next chapter, "Stored Procedures and Parameters," will show how you can save multiple SQL statements in a procedure and make use of parameters within those procedures to add a degree of generality to SQL commands. We'll also talk about the possibility of creating your own custom functions, and explain how functions differ from stored procedures. Much like the views discussed in Chapter 13, "Self Joins and Views," stored procedures and custom functions are useful objects that you can create and store in your database to provide some extra polish and functionality.

16

Stored Procedures and Parameters

Keywords Introduced

CREATE PROCEDURE · BEGIN · EXEC/CALL · ALTER PROCEDURE · DROP PROCEDURE

Up until this point, all of our data retrieval has been accomplished with a single SQL statement. Even the set logic seen in the previous chapter involved combining multiple SELECTs into a single statement. Now we'll discuss a new scenario, in which multiple statements can be saved into a single object known as a *stored procedure*.

In broad terms, there are two general reasons for using stored procedures:

- To save multiple SQL statements in a single procedure
- To use parameters in conjunction with SQL statements

Stored procedures can, in fact, consist of a single SQL statement and contain no parameters. But the real value of stored procedures becomes evident when they contain multiple statements or parameters.

The subject of stored procedures is quite complex. In this brief review of the topic, we'll focus on an overview of the second stated reason, that of using parameters. This relates directly to the issue of how best to retrieve data from a database. As we'll see, the ability to add parameters to a SELECT statement turns out to be a very useful feature in everyday usage.

The use of stored procedures to contain multiple statements is beyond the scope of this book. Basically, the ability to store multiple statements in a procedure means that you can create complex logic and execute it all at once in a single transaction. For example, you might have a business requirement to take an incoming order from a customer and quickly evaluate it before allowing it to enter the system. This procedure might involve checking to make sure that the items are in stock, verifying that the customer has a good credit rating, and getting an initial estimate as to when the items can be shipped. This situation would require multiple SQL statements with some added logic to determine what kind of message to return if all is not well with the order. All of that logic can be placed into a single stored procedure. This enhances the modularity of the entire system. With everything in one procedure, that logic can be executed from any calling program and return the same result.

Creating Stored Procedures

Before we get into the details of how to use stored procedures, let's cover the mechanics of how they are created and maintained. The syntax varies significantly among different databases. For Microsoft SQL Server, the general format for creating a stored procedure is:

```
CREATE PROCEDURE ProcedureName
AS
OptionalParameterDeclarations
BEGIN
SQLStatements
END
```

The CREATE PROCEDURE keyword allows you to issue a single command that creates the procedure. The procedure itself can contain any number of SQL statements and can also contain parameter declarations. We'll discuss the parameter declaration syntax later. The SQL statements are listed between the BEGIN and END keywords.

Database Differences: MySQL and Oracle

The general format for creating a stored procedure in MySQL is slightly more complex. The MySQL format is:

```
DELIMITER $$
CREATE PROCEDURE ProcedureName ()
BEGIN
SQLStatements
END$$
DELIMITER ;
```

MySQL requires delimiters when executing multiple statements. The normal delimiter is a semicolon. The first line in the above code temporarily changes the standard delimiter from a semicolon to two dollar signs. Any needed parameters are specified between the parentheses on the CREATE PROCEDURE line. Then each SQL statement listed between the BEGIN and END keywords must have a semicolon at the end of the statement. The dollar signs are written after the END keyword to denote that the CREATE PROCEDURE command is completed. Finally, another DELIMITER statement is placed at the end to change the delimiter back to a semicolon.

The procedure for creating stored procedures in Oracle is quite a bit more involved and is beyond the scope of this book. To create a stored procedure for a SELECT statement in Oracle, you must first create an object called a package. The package will contain two basic components: a specification and a body. The specification component specifies how to communicate with the body component. The body component contains the SQL statements, which are at the heart of the stored procedure. Consult Oracle's online documentation for further details.

Here's an example of how to create a stored procedure that can be used to execute this single SELECT statement:

```
SELECT *
FROM Customers
```

The procedure will be named ProcedureOne. In Microsoft SQL Server, the statement to create the procedure is:

```
CREATE PROCEDURE ProcedureOne
AS
BEGIN
SELECT *
FROM Customers
END
```

Database Differences: MySQL

In MySQL, the previous example would look like:

```
DELIMITER $$
CREATE PROCEDURE ProcedureName ()
BEGIN
SELECT *
FROM Customers;
END$$
DELIMITER ;
```

Remember that creating a stored procedure does not execute anything. It simply creates the procedure so it can be executed later. Along with tables and views, the procedure will be visible in your database management tool, allowing you to view its contents.

Parameters in Stored Procedures

All of the SELECT statements we have seen up until now have had a certain static quality due to the fact that they were written to retrieve data in one specific way. The ability to add parameters to SELECT statements provides the possibility of much greater flexibility.

The term *parameter* in SQL statements is similar to the term *variable* as it is used in other computer languages. A parameter is basically a value passed to a SQL statement by the calling program. It can have whatever value the user specifies at the time the call is made.

Starting with a simple example, let's say we have a SELECT statement that retrieves data from a Customers table. Rather than selecting all customers, we would like the SELECT to retrieve data for only one specific CustomerID number. However, we don't want to code the number directly in the SELECT statement. We want the SELECT to be general enough that it can accept any provided CustomerID number and then execute with that value. The SELECT statement without any parameters is simply:

```
SELECT *
FROM Customers
```

Our goal is to add a WHERE clause that allows us to select data for a particular customer. In a general form, we'd like the SELECT statement to be:

```
SELECT *
FROM Customers
WHERE CustomerID = ParameterValue
```

In Microsoft SQL Server, the creation of such a stored procedure can be accomplished with this:

```
CREATE PROCEDURE CustomerProcedure
(@CustID INT)
AS
BEGIN
SELECT *
FROM Customers
WHERE CustomerID = @CustID
END
```

Notice the addition of the second line, which specifies the CustID parameter in the procedure. In Microsoft SQL Server, the @ symbol is used to denote a parameter. The INT keyword is placed after the parameter to indicate that this parameter will have an integer value. The same parameter name is used in the WHERE clause.

Database Differences: MySQL

In MySQL, the command to create an equivalent stored procedure is:

```
DELIMITER $$
CREATE PROCEDURE CustomerProcedure
(CustID INT)
BEGIN
SELECT *
FROM Customers
WHERE CustomerID = CustID;
END$$
DELIMITER ;
```

Notice that MySQL doesn't require the @ symbol to denote a parameter.

When a stored procedure is executed, the calling program passes a value for the parameter, and the SQL statement is executed as if that value were part of the statement.

Also note that the parameters discussed previously are input parameters. As such, they contain values that are passed into the stored procedure. Stored procedures can also include output parameters, which can contain values passed back to the calling program. It's beyond the scope of this book to discuss the various nuances of how to specify both input and output parameters in stored procedures.

Executing Stored Procedures

After stored procedures are created, how are they executed? The syntax varies between databases. Microsoft SQL Server provides the EXEC keyword to run stored procedures.

In Microsoft SQL Server, the following statement will execute the ProcedureOne procedure:

```
EXEC ProcedureOne
```

When this statement is executed, it returns the results of the SELECT statement contained in the stored procedure.

The ProcedureOne parameter didn't have any parameters, so the syntax is simple. To illustrate running procedures with input parameters, the following executes the CustomerProcedure procedure for a CustID value of 2:

```
EXEC CustomerProcedure
@CustID = 2
```

Database Differences: MySQL

Rather than using EXEC, MySQL uses a CALL keyword to execute stored procedures, and the syntax for stored procedures with parameters is slightly different. The equivalent of the previous two EXEC statements in MySQL is:

```
CALL ProcedureOne:
CALL CustomerProcedure (2);
```

Modifying and Deleting Stored Procedures

Once a stored procedure has been created, it can be modified. Just as the ALTER keyword was used to modify views, the ALTER PROCEDURE keyword is used to modify stored procedures. The syntax is identical to the CREATE PROCEDURE command, except that ALTER is used in place of CREATE. Just as the CREATE PROCEDURE has a slightly different syntax for each database, so does the ALTER PROCEDURE.

We've already seen this example of creating a stored procedure with Microsoft SQL Server:

```
CREATE PROCEDURE CustomerProcedure
(@CustID INT)
AS
BEGIN
SELECT *
FROM Customers
WHERE CustomerID = @CustID
END
```

After this procedure is created, if you wanted to alter the procedure to select only the CustomerID and LastName columns from the Customers table, the command to accomplish that would be:

```
ALTER PROCEDURE CustomerProcedure
(@CustID INT)
AS
BEGIN
SELECT
CustomerID,
LastName
FROM Customers
WHERE CustomerID = @CustID
END
```

Database Differences: MySQL

MySQL provides an ALTER PROCEDURE command, but it has limited functionality. To alter the content of a stored procedure in MySQL, you need to issue a DROP PROCEDURE and then a CREATE PROCEDURE with the new content.

Deleting a stored procedure is even simpler. Just as the DROP VIEW deletes a view, the DROP PROCEDURE statement deletes a procedure.

Here's how the stored procedure named CustomerProcedure can be deleted:

```
DROP PROCEDURE CustomerProcedure
```

Functions Revisited

In Chapter 4, we talked about the built-in scalar functions available in SQL. For example, we used character functions such as LEFT and mathematical functions like ROUND. In Chapter 9, we discussed aggregate functions such as MAX.

In addition to the built-in functions in SQL, developers can create their own functions and save them in a database. The procedure for creating functions is very similar to the procedure for creating stored procedures. SQL provides the keywords CREATE FUNCTION, ALTER FUNCTION, and DROP FUNCTION, which work very much like CREATE PROCEDURE, ALTER PROCEDURE, and DROP PROCEDURE.

Due to the advanced nature of this topic, we won't provide specific examples of this functionality. However, we'll spend a few moments explaining the differences between using stored procedures and functions.

Both stored procedures and functions can be saved in a database. These entities are saved as separate objects in a database, much like tables or views. The procedures for saving and modifying stored procedures and functions are very similar. The same CREATE, ALTER, and DROP commands for stored procedures can be used for functions.

The difference between the two lies in how they are used and in their capabilities. There are two main distinctions between stored procedures and functions:

- **Stored procedures can have any number of output parameters.** They can even have zero output parameters. In contrast, a function must always contain exactly one output parameter. In other words, when you call a function, you always get back a single value.
- **Stored procedures are executed by a calling program.** The stored procedure cannot be directly referenced in a SELECT statement. In contrast, functions can be referenced within statements, as seen in Chapters 4 and 9. After a function is defined, that function is referenced by the name specified when it was created.

Looking Ahead

In this chapter, we've seen that the use of parameters can add a great deal of flexibility to the process of retrieving data. For example, parameters allow us to generalize SQL statements so that values for selection criteria can be specified at the time the statement is executed. We also learned about the basics of how to create and modify stored procedures. Finally, we explained some of the differences between stored procedures and user-defined functions.

Although the examples in this chapter focused on data retrieval, stored procedures and functions are also quite useful for applying data updates. Our next chapter, "Modifying Data," will take us completely out of the realm of data retrieval and move us squarely into issues surrounding the need to update data. The business of maintaining data doesn't present the same analytic possibilities as data retrieval, but it is a necessary task for any enterprise. Fortunately, most of the techniques we've learned with the SELECT statement apply equally to the modification process discussed in the next chapter.

17

Modifying Data

Keywords Introduced

INSERT INTO · VALUES · DELETE · TRUNCATE TABLE · UPDATE · SET

Having exhausted our discussion of retrieving data from databases, we now move on to the question of how to modify data in a database. There are three basic scenarios as to how data can be modified:

- Inserting new rows into a table
- Deleting rows from a table
- Updating existing data in specific rows and columns in a table

As may be surmised, inserting and deleting rows is relatively straightforward. Updating existing data, however, is a more complex endeavor, as it involves identifying the rows to be updated and also the specific columns in those rows. We'll begin with the inserts and deletes and then move on to updates.

Modification Strategies

The mechanics of modifying data are fairly straightforward. However, the nature of the process means that this is an area fraught with peril. Being human, mistakes can be made. With a single command, you can easily delete thousands of rows in error or apply incorrect updates that may be difficult to retract.

As a practical matter, various strategies can be employed to help prevent catastrophic blunders. For example, when deleting rows from a table, you can employ a *soft delete* technique. This means that instead of actually deleting rows, you denote a special column in a table that marks each row as either active or inactive. Rather than deleting a row, you merely mark it as inactive. That way, if a deletion is done in error, you can easily reverse it by changing the value of the active/inactive status column.

A similar technique can be used when doing inserts. When adding a row, you can mark the exact date and time of the insert in a special column. If it is later determined that the row was added in error, you can find all rows that were added within a specified time range and have them deleted.

The problem is more complex when it comes to updating data. Generally, it's advisable to maintain a separate table that holds data on intended update transactions. If any kind of error is made, you can go back to the transaction table to find the before and after values for data that was modified and use that to reverse any earlier mistakes.

The aforementioned strategies are just a few of the many approaches you can take. This topic is well beyond the scope of this book. The bottom line is to exercise caution when updating data. Unlike many user-friendly desktop applications, SQL has no undo command.

Inserting Data

SQL provides an INSERT keyword for adding data into a table. There are two basic ways an INSERT can be done:

- Insert specific data listed in an INSERT statement
- Insert data obtained from a SELECT statement

Let's start with an example that shows how to insert data, where the data values are specified in the INSERT statement. We'll assume that we have a Clients table with this data already in it:

ClientID	FirstName	LastName	State
1	Joyce	Bentley	TN
2	Miguel	Ramirez	PA
3	Ellen	Baker	OR

Let's also assume that the first column, ClientID, is the primary key for the table. Back in Chapters 1 and 2, we talked about the fact that primary keys enforce the requirement that each row in a table be uniquely identifiable. We also mentioned that primary key columns are often specified as auto-increment columns. This means that they are automatically assigned a number as rows are added to the table.

Assuming that the ClientID is defined as an auto-increment column, this means that when we add a row to the Clients table, we don't need to specify a value for the ClientID column. It will be automatically determined as each row is added to the table. We need only to specify values for the other three columns.

Let's proceed with a procedure that adds two new customers to the table: Claudia Davis from Ohio and Ingrid Krause from California. This statement performs the insert:

```
INSERT INTO Clients
(FirstName, LastName, State)
VALUES
('Claudia', 'Davis', 'OH'),
('Ingrid', 'Krause', 'CA')
```

After the insert, the table contains:

ClientID	FirstName	LastName	State
1	Joyce	Bentley	TN
2	Miguel	Ramirez	PA
3	Ellen	Baker	OR
4	Claudia	Davis	OH
5	Ingrid	Krause	CA

A few words of explanation are in order. First, notice that the VALUES keyword is used as a prefix to lists of values to be inserted into the table. The statement lists each row of data in a separate set of parentheses. Claudia Davis of Ohio was in one set of parentheses; Ingrid Krause was in another set. The two sets were separated by a comma. If we needed to add only one row, then just one set of parentheses would be needed.

Database Differences: Oracle

Oracle doesn't support auto-increment columns.

Also, Oracle doesn't permit multiple rows to be specified after the VALUES keyword. The previous example would need to be broken down into two statements, as follows:

```
INSERT INTO Clients
(FirstName, LastName, State)
VALUES
('Claudia', 'Davis', 'OH');

INSERT INTO Clients
(FirstName, LastName, State)
VALUES
('Ingrid', 'Krause', 'CA');
```

Also note that the order of the data elements after the VALUES keyword corresponds to the order of columns listed in the *columnlist* after the INSERT INTO. The order in which the columns themselves are listed does not have to be the same as in the database. In other words, the above insert could have been accomplished just as easily with this statement:

```
INSERT INTO Clients
(State, LastName, FirstName)
VALUES
('OH', 'Davis', 'Claudia'),
('CA', 'Krause', 'Ingrid')
```

In this INSERT, we listed the State column first instead of last. Again, the order in which columns are listed doesn't matter.

To sum up, the general format for the INSERT INTO statement is:

```
INSERT INTO table
(columnlist)
VALUES
(RowValues1),
(RowValues2)
[repeat any number of times]
```

The columns in the *columnlist* must correspond to the columns in *RowValues*.

Also, if all the columns in the columnlist are listed in the same order as they physically exist in the database, and if there are no auto-increment columns in the table, then the INSERT INTO statement can be executed without specifying the *columnlist*. However, this practice is strongly discouraged because it is prone to error.

It's also possible to use an INSERT statement without specifying all the columns. When that occurs, columns not specified are given NULL values. For example, let's say we want to insert one additional row into the Clients table for a customer named Deepak Gupta. However, we don't know Deepak's state. Here's the INSERT:

```
INSERT INTO Clients
(FirstName, LastName)
VALUES
('Deepak', 'Gupta')
```

Afterward, his row in the table will appear as:

ClientID	FirstName	LastName	State
6	Deepak	Gupta	NULL

Because we didn't specify a value for the State column for this new row, it was given a NULL value.

There are two variations of the INSERT INTO statement. The second format applies to situations where you insert data obtained from a SELECT statement. This means that instead of listing data elements after a VALUES keyword, you substitute a SELECT statement that obtains the necessary values.

To illustrate, let's say we have another table named NewClients, which holds data that we would like to insert into the Clients table. The NewClients table might look like this:

State	Name1	Name2
RI	Roberto	Harris
PA	Beata	Kowalski
RI	Galina	Melnyk

If we would like to add all customers from the state of Rhode Island (RI) from the NewClients table to the Clients table, the following would accomplish that objective:

```
INSERT INTO Clients
(FirstName, LastName, State)
SELECT
Name1,
Name2,
State
FROM NewClients
WHERE State = 'RI'
```

After this INSERT, the Clients table contains:

ClientID	FirstName	LastName	State
1	Joyce	Bentley	TN
2	Miguel	Ramirez	PA
3	Ellen	Baker	OR
4	Claudia	Davis	OH
5	Ingrid	Krause	CA
6	Deepak	Gupta	NULL
7	Roberto	Harris	RI
8	Galina	Melnyk	RI

The above INSERT simply substitutes a SELECT statement for the VALUES clause. As would be expected, Beata Kowalski didn't get added to the Clients table because she is not in Rhode Island. Also notice that the column names in the Clients and NewClients tables are not identical. The column names don't matter as long as the columns are listed in the correct corresponding order.

Deleting Data

Deleting data is quite a bit simpler than adding it. The DELETE statement is used to handle deletions. When a DELETE is executed, it removes entire rows, not individual columns in a row. The general format is:

```
DELETE
FROM table
WHERE condition
```

Here's a simple example. Let's say we want to delete rows from the previously mentioned Clients table if the customer is in Rhode Island. The statement to accomplish this is:

```
DELETE
FROM Clients
WHERE State = 'RI'
```

That's all there is to it. If you wanted to test the results of the previous DELETE before executing it, you could simply substitute a SELECT for the DELETE, as follows:

```
SELECT
COUNT(*)
FROM Clients
WHERE State = 'RI'
```

This would provide a count of the rows about to be deleted, which supplies some level of validation for the delete.

There is one other option for deleting data that is worth mentioning. If you want to delete all the data in a single column, you can employ a TRUNCATE TABLE statement to delete everything. The advantage of the TRUNCATE TABLE over the DELETE statement is that it is much faster. Unlike the DELETE, the TRUNCATE TABLE doesn't log the results of the transaction. We haven't talked about data log processes, but this is a function that most databases provide that allows database administrators to recover databases in the event of system crashes and other similar problems.

If you want to delete all rows in the Clients table, you can issue this statement:

```
TRUNCATE TABLE Clients
```

This has the same result as this statement:

```
DELETE
FROM Clients
```

One other slight difference between the DELETE and the TRUNCATE TABLE is that the TRUNCATE TABLE resets the values used for auto-increment columns. The DELETE doesn't affect those values.

Updating Data

The procedure for updating data involves specifying which columns are to be updated, as well as logic for selecting rows. The general format for an UPDATE statement is:

```
UPDATE table
SET Column1 = Expression1,
Column2 = Expression2
[repeat any number of times]
WHERE condition
```

This statement is similar to the basic SELECT, except that the SET keyword is used to assign new values for specified columns. The WHERE condition specifies which rows are to be updated, but the UPDATE statement can update multiple columns at the same time. If more than one column is being updated, the SET keyword is listed only once, but a comma must separate all update expressions.

Starting with a simple example, let's say we want to change Joyce Bentley's last name to Barrow, and also change her state from Tennessee (TN) to Wisconsin (WI). Her row in the Clients table currently looks like this:

ClientID	FirstName	LastName	State
1	Joyce	Bentley	TN

The UPDATE statement to accomplish the modification is:

```
UPDATE Clients
SET LastName = 'Barrow',
State = 'WI'
WHERE ClientID = 1
```

After executing this statement, this row in the Clients table has been changed to:

ClientID	FirstName	LastName	State
1	Joyce	Barrow	WI

Notice that the value of the FirstName column is unchanged because that column wasn't included in the UPDATE statement. Also note that the WHERE clause is essential. Without the WHERE, this change would have been applied to every row in the table.

Correlated Subquery Updates

The previous UPDATE example is easy enough but not entirely realistic. A more common use of an UPDATE involves situations in which you update data in one table based on data in another table. Let's say we have this Vendors table:

VendorID	State	Zip
1	NY	10605
2	FL	33431
3	CA	94704
4	CO	80302
5	WY	83001

This VendorTransactions table includes recent changes for existing vendors:

TransactionID	VendorID	State	Zip
1	1	NJ	07030
2	2	FL	33139
3	5	OR	97401

The Vendors table is the main source of data for vendors. To accomplish an update of the Vendors table from the VendorTransactions table, we'll need to use the subquery technique discussed in Chapter 14. The correlated subquery is needed because the UPDATE statement can only specify a single table to update. We can't merely join multiple tables together and have it work. We'll need to use a correlated subquery after the SET keyword to indicate where the data comes from.

The following statement can be used to update the State and Zip columns in the Vendors table from the transactions in the VendorTransactions table. Because this statement is fairly complex, we've inserted a few blank lines so we can subsequently discuss the four sections of the statement.

```
UPDATE Vendors

SET Vendors.State =
(SELECT VendorTransactions.State
FROM VendorTransactions
WHERE Vendors.VendorID = VendorTransactions.VendorID),

Vendors.Zip =
(SELECT VendorTransactions.Zip
FROM VendorTransactions
WHERE Vendors.VendorID = VendorTransactions.VendorID)

WHERE EXISTS
(SELECT *
FROM VendorTransactions
WHERE Vendors.VendorID = VendorTransactions.VendorID)
```

Let's analyze this UPDATE statement in some detail. The first section of the statement, consisting of the first line, indicates that the update is to be done on the Vendors table.

The second section of the statement specifies how the State column is to be updated. The update is based on this correlated subquery:

```
SELECT VendorTransactions.State
FROM VendorTransactions
WHERE Vendors.VendorID = VendorTransactions.VendorID
```

We can tell that this is a correlated subquery because it would produce an error if we attempted to execute this SELECT on its own. The subquery is taking data from the VendorTransactions table and matching between the two tables by VendorID.

The third section of the statement is identical to the second section, except that these lines are concerned with updates to the Zip column. Also notice that the SET keyword only needed to be specified once, in the second section. It isn't needed in the third section.

The final section includes logic in a WHERE clause associated with the selection logic for the entire UPDATE statement. The EXISTS operator is used along with another correlated subquery to determine whether rows exist in the VendorTransactions table for each VendorID in the Vendors table. Without this WHERE clause, the update would incorrectly change the State and Zip columns for vendors 3 and 4 to NULL values, because those vendors do not have rows in the VendorTransactions table. The correlated subquery in this WHERE clause makes certain that we apply updates only for vendors who do, in fact, have data in the VendorTransactions table.

As you can infer, the subject of using correlated subqueries for updates is quite complex. As such, the topic is generally beyond the scope of this book. We've included this example merely to give an idea of some of the complexities involved in data updates. Additionally, note that correlated subqueries are similarly useful with deletes.

Looking Ahead

This chapter presented an overview of the various methods of updating data. The mechanics of executing simple inserts, deletes, and updates are relatively straightforward. However, the correlated subquery technique, which is often necessary for real-world updates and deletes, is not for the faint of heart. Additionally, the entire notion of applying updates to data is a demanding exercise. With the power of SQL's ability to update thousands of rows of data with a single command comes an admonition to exercise caution when performing any type of update. Procedures for reversing any updates should be carefully planned out before any data modifications are applied.

Now that we've talked about modifying the data in tables, we progress next to a discussion of the tables themselves. In our next chapter, "Maintaining Tables," we'll look at the mechanics of creating tables, along with all the attributes needed to properly hold the data in those tables. As such, we'll be revisiting some of the topics touched upon in Chapter 1, such as primary and foreign keys. Up until now, we've assumed that tables are simply available for our use. After this examination, you'll have a much better idea of how to create the tables that will hold your data.

18

Maintaining Tables

Keywords Introduced

CREATE TABLE · DROP TABLE · CREATE INDEX · DROP INDEX

With this chapter, we change our focus from data retrieval and modification to design. Up until now, we've assumed that tables simply exist and are available to any interested user. However, in the normal course of events, someone must create tables before the data in them can be accessed. We now turn to the question of how to create and maintain tables.

We previously touched on a few of the topics we'll be addressing, such as primary and foreign keys, but we now want to delve into these areas in greater detail, and also bring in the related topic of table indexes.

Data Definition Language

Way back in Chapter 1, we mentioned the three main components of the SQL language: DML (Data Manipulation Language), DDL (Data Definition Language), and DCL (Data Control Language). Up until now, most of what we've talked about has been DML. DML statements allow you to manipulate data in relational databases by retrieval, insertion, deletion, or updating. This is handled by the SELECT, INSERT, DELETE, and UPDATE statements.

Although our focus has been on DML, we have already seen a few instances of DDL (Data Definition Language). The CREATE VIEW and CREATE PROCEDURE statements we encountered in Chapters 13 and 16 are DDL, as are the related ALTER and DROP versions of those statements.

CREATE VIEW and CREATE PROCEDURE statements are DDL because they only allow you to manipulate the structure of the database. They have nothing to do with the data in databases.

In this chapter, we'll provide a brief overview of a few additional DDL statements that can be used to create and modify tables and indexes.

Each database has a different way of organizing its objects, and therefore has different available DDL statements. For example, MySQL has 11 different CREATE statements for these types of objects: Databases, Events, Functions, Indexes, Logfile Groups, Procedures, Servers, Tables, TableSpaces, Triggers, and Views.

Oracle has more than 30 different CREATE commands for the object types in its database. Microsoft SQL Server has more than 40 different CREATE commands for its object types.

In truth, most modifications to database objects, such as views and tables, can be accomplished through the visual GUI (graphical user interface) that each software vendor provides to administer their software. It is often not necessary to learn any DDL at all, because it can often be handled with the software GUI.

However, it's useful to be aware of at least the existence of a few key statements for manipulating data objects. We've already seen some statements that allow us to modify views and stored procedures. In this chapter, we'll cover some of the possibilities for modifying tables and indexes via DDL.

Table Attributes

In the first two chapters, we briefly discussed a few attributes of database tables, such as primary keys, foreign keys, datatypes, and auto-increment columns. As mentioned, SQL DDL provides CREATE statements for many types of database objects. In Chapters 13 and 16, we talked about the CREATE PROCEDURE and CREATE VIEW statements that handle stored procedures and views.

We'll now bring our attention back to tables. Tables are perhaps the primary and most essential object type in a database. Without tables, nothing else really matters. All the data in a database is physically stored in tables. Most other object types relate to tables in one way or another. Views provide a virtual view of tables. Stored procedures generally act upon data in tables. Functions allow for special rules for the manipulation of data in tables.

We'll focus here on how tables can be created initially. A large number of attributes can be associated with table definitions. We'll give an overview of some of the more important attributes and discuss what they mean.

The subject of table attributes is also related to the larger topic of database design, which will be addressed in the next chapter. For now, we want to focus on the mechanics of what can be done with the tables themselves.

The specifics of how tables can be designed and altered varies widely among Microsoft SQL Server, MySQL, and Oracle. We'll talk primarily about those attributes common to tables in all three databases.

Table Columns

Tables are defined as containing any number of columns. Each column has a variety of attributes specific to that column. The first and most obvious attribute is the column name. Each column must be given a name unique to that table.

A second attribute of columns is the datatype, a subject that was addressed in Chapter 1. We've already described some notable datatypes in three main categories: numeric, character, and date/time. The datatype is a key determinant of the type of data each column can contain.

A third attribute of columns is whether or not it can be defined as an auto-increment column. We briefly introduced this attribute type in Chapters 1 and 2 and discussed it further in the preceding chapter about modifying data. Basically, an auto-increment column means that the column is automatically assigned a numeric value, in ascending sequence, as each row is added to the table. Auto-increment columns are often used with primary keys but can also be assigned to an ordinary column.

Note that the term *auto-increment* is specific to MySQL. Microsoft uses the term *identity* to refer to the same type of attribute.

Database Differences: Oracle

Oracle doesn't have an auto-increment type of attribute. Instead, Oracle requires you to define a column as a *sequence* and then create a *trigger* to populate that column with sequential values. This procedure is beyond the scope of this book.

A fourth column attribute is whether or not the column is allowed to contain NULL values. The default is to allow NULL values. If you don't want to allow a column to contain NULLs, it is normally specified via a NOT NULL keyword applied to the column description.

The final column attribute we'll mention is whether the column is assigned a default value. A default value is automatically assigned to the column if no value for that column is provided when a row is added. For example, if most of your customers are in the US, you may want to specify that a column containing a country code be given a default value of US.

Primary Keys and Indexes

Let's turn to the topic of primary keys and explain how that attribute relates to table indexes.

Indexes are a physical structure that can be added to any column in a database table. Indexes serve the purpose of speeding up data retrieval when that column is involved in a SQL statement. The actual data in the index is hidden, but basically the index involves a structure that maintains information on the sort order of the column, thus allowing for quicker retrieval when specific values are requested.

One downside to indexing a column is that it requires more disk storage in the database. A second negative is that indexes generally slow down data updates involving that column. This happens because any time a row is inserted or modified, the index must recalculate the proper sorted order for values in that column.

Any column can be indexed, but only one column can be designated as a primary key. Specifying a column as a primary key means two things: The column will be indexed, and the column will be guaranteed to contain unique values.

As discussed in Chapter 1, primary keys accomplish two main benefits for the database user. They enable you to uniquely identify a single row in a table, and they allow you to easily relate tables to one another. And now, a third benefit can be added—namely, that by being indexed, the primary key enables faster data retrieval of rows involving that column.

The main reason for having primary keys is to guarantee unique values for all rows in a table. There must always be a way of identifying single rows for updates or deletes, and the primary key ensures that this can be done.

Moreover, a primary key can actually span more than one column and can consist of two or three columns. If the primary key contains more than one column, it simply means that all those columns together will contain a unique value. This type of primary key is normally referred to as a *composite primary key*. As an example of when a composite primary key might be used, let's say that you have a Movies table. You'd like to have a key that uniquely identifies each movie in the table. Rather than using a MovieID integer value as the key, you'd like to use the movie title as the key. The problem, however, is that there might exist more than one movie with the same title. To solve the problem, you might want to use two columns—the movie title and the release date—to form a composite primary to uniquely define each movie.

Because primary keys must contain unique values, they are never allowed to contain NULL values. Some value for the column must always be specified.

Finally, primary keys are often specified as auto-increment columns. By making a primary key auto-increment, database developers don't need to worry about assigning a unique value for the column. The auto-increment feature takes care of that requirement.

Foreign Keys

SQL databases can also designate specific columns as a foreign key. A foreign key is simply a reference from a column in one table to a column in a different table. When setting up a foreign key, you will be asked to specify both columns. The foreign key in the table being configured is often referred to as being in the *child table*. The referenced column in the other table is referred to as being in the *parent table*.

For example, let's say you have a Customers table with a CustomerID column set up as a primary key. You also have an Orders table with an OrderID column set up as a primary key, as well as a CustomerID column. In this scenario, you can set up the CustomerID column in the

Orders table as a foreign key that references the CustomerID column in the Customers table. In this situation, the Orders table is the child table and the Customers table is the parent table. The idea of the foreign key is to ensure that the CustomerID in the Orders table points to an existing customer in the Customers table, using the CustomerID column in both tables as the common element.

When a foreign key is set up, some specific actions can be set up pertaining to updates and deletes for rows in the parent table. The three most common actions are:

- No Action
- Cascade
- Set Null

These three actions can be specified for either updates or deletes. Continuing with the example of the Customers and Orders tables, the most common action that might be specified is *No Action*. This is normally the default action if none is specified. If the CustomerID column in the Orders table is set to No Action for updates, that means that a check is made whenever an update is attempted in the parent table on the CustomerID column. If SQL tries to perform an update on the CustomerID that would result in any row in the child table pointing to a value that no longer exists, it will prevent that action from occurring. The same would be true if No Action is specified for deletes. This ensures that, when using the CustomerID column in either table, all rows in the Orders table properly point to an existing row in the Customers table.

The second alternative for a specified action for foreign keys is *Cascade*. This means that when a value in the parent table is updated, and that value affects rows in the child table, then SQL will automatically update all rows in the child table to reflect the new value in the parent table. Similarly, if a row in the parent table is deleted, and if that affects rows in the child table, SQL will automatically delete affected rows in the child table.

The third alternative for a specified action for foreign keys is *Set Null*, which is sometimes used for deletes. This means that when a value in the parent table is deleted, and if that value affects rows in the child table, SQL will automatically update all affected rows in the child table to contain a NULL value in the foreign key, indicating that a corresponding parent row doesn't exist.

Creating Tables

The CREATE TABLE statement can be used to create new tables in a database. The syntax and available features vary among databases. We'll illustrate this with a simple example that creates a table with these attributes:

- The table name is MyTable.
- The first column in the table is named ColumnOne and is defined as a primary key. This column will be defined as an INT (integer) datatype and also as an auto-increment column.

- The second column in the table is named ColumnTwo and is defined as an INT datatype. This column will not allow NULL values. This column will also be defined as a foreign key, with Set Null specified for deletes, related to a column named FirstColumn in another table called RelatedTable.
- The third column is named ColumnThree and is defined as a VARCHAR datatype with a length of 25 characters. This column will allow NULL values.
- The fourth column is named ColumnFour, is defined as a FLOAT datatype, and will allow NULL values. It will be given a default value of 10.

Here is the CREATE TABLE statement that will create such a table in Microsoft SQL Server:

```
CREATE TABLE MyTable
(ColumnOne INT IDENTITY(1,1) PRIMARY KEY NOT NULL,
ColumnTwo INT NULL
REFERENCES RelatedTable (FirstColumn)
ON DELETE SET NULL,
ColumnThree VARCHAR(25) NULL,
ColumnFour FLOAT NULL DEFAULT (10))
```

Database Differences: MySQL and Oracle

The same CREATE TABLE statement in MySQL looks like this:

```
CREATE TABLE MyTable
(ColumnOne INT AUTO_INCREMENT PRIMARY KEY NOT NULL,
ColumnTwo INT NULL,
ColumnThree VARCHAR(25) NULL,
ColumnFour FLOAT NULL DEFAULT 10,
CONSTRAINT FOREIGN KEY(ColumnTwo)
REFERENCES RelatedTable (FirstColumn)
ON DELETE SET NULL);
```

The same statement in Oracle is:

```
CREATE TABLE MyTable
(ColumnOne INT PRIMARY KEY NOT NULL,
ColumnTwo INT NULL,
ColumnThree VARCHAR(25) NULL,
ColumnFour FLOAT DEFAULT 10 NULL,
CONSTRAINT "ForeignKey" FOREIGN KEY (ColumnTwo)
REFERENCES RelatedTable (FirstColumn)
ON DELETE SET NULL);
```

As previously mentioned, Oracle doesn't allow for auto-increment columns.

After a table is created, an ALTER TABLE statement can be used to modify specific attributes of the table. Due to its complexity and to the vast differences between databases for this command, the syntax for the ALTER TABLE isn't covered in this book.

As one example, the following statement could be used to modify MyTable to eliminate the ColumnThree column from the table:

```
ALTER TABLE MyTable
DROP COLUMN ColumnThree
```

The syntax for deleting an entire table is simple. To delete MyTable, issue this statement:

```
DROP TABLE MyTable
```

Creating Indexes

SQL provides a CREATE INDEX statement for creating indexes after the table is created. You can also use the ALTER TABLE statement to add or modify indexes.

To illustrate, the syntax in Microsoft SQL Server for adding a new index on ColumnFour in MyTable is:

```
CREATE INDEX Index2
ON MyTable(ColumnFour)
```

This creates a new index named Index2. To delete an index, simply issue a DROP INDEX statement such as:

```
DROP INDEX Index2
ON MyTable
```

Database Differences: Oracle

In Oracle, the equivalent DROP INDEX statement is:
```
DROP INDEX Index2;
```

Looking Ahead

The SQL statements for adding or modifying tables and indexes are complex but relatively unimportant to learn in detail. Database software generally provides graphical tools for modifying the structure of tables without having to resort to issuing SQL statements. The important concepts to take from this chapter are a knowledge of the various table attributes, including an understanding of how indexes and primary and foreign keys are related to each other.

In our next chapter, "Principles of Database Design," we move from the relatively mundane task of creating tables to the much broader topic of database design. Just as tables must be created before their data is accessed, the overall structure of databases is normally designed before tables are created. So, in a sense, we're moving in reverse through topics that are normally introduced before retrieval of data is ever attempted. The specific design of your database is, of course, an essential component of your ability to deliver quality results via SQL. If a database is poorly designed, anyone accessing data in that database will be hindered in their attempts to retrieve data. Basic knowledge of the database design principles discussed in the next chapter can go a long way toward ensuring a quality data retrieval experience.

19

Principles of Database Design

In our first chapter, we introduced the notion that relational databases are a collection of data, stored in any number of tables. The tables are assumed to be related to each other in some fashion. In the previous chapter, on maintaining tables, we made clear that database designers can, if they choose, assign foreign keys to ensure that certain relationships between tables are maintained properly.

However, even with our knowledge of primary and foreign keys, we still have not yet addressed the basic issue of how to design a database in the first place. The main questions to address are the following:

- How should data be organized into a set of related tables?
- What data elements should be placed in each table?

Once tables and their data elements are defined, then a database administrator can go about the business of creating foreign keys, indexes, appropriate datatypes, and so on.

There will never be a single correct answer to the above two questions. Besides the fact that every organization or business is unique, there is seldom a definitive solution for any given situation. Much depends on how flexible a business wants its data design to be. Another factor is the existence of current data and the need to maintain continuity with that data. Very few organizations have the luxury of designing their databases in a vacuum, apart from what already exists.

Despite these provisions, certain database design principles have evolved over time to guide us in our quest for an optimal design structure. Many of these design principles stem from the most influential architect of relational database design, E.F. Codd, who published his groundbreaking article "A Relational Model of Data for Large Shared Data Banks" in 1979. This article laid the foundation for what we now call the *relational model* and the concept of *normalization*.

Goals of Normalization

The term *normalization* refers to a specific process that allows database architects to turn unstructured data into a properly designed set of tables and data elements.

The best way to understand normalization is to illustrate what it isn't. To do this, we'll start with the presentation of a poorly designed table with a number of obvious problems. The following is a table named Grades, which attempts to present information about all the grades that students have received for the tests they've taken. Each row represents a grade for a particular student.

Test	Student	Date	TotalPoints	Grade	TestFormat	Teacher	Assistant
Pronoun Quiz	Amy	2017-03-02	10	8	Multiple Choice	Smith	Collins
Pronoun Quiz	Jon	2017-03-02	10	6	Multiple Choice	Jones	Brown
Solids Quiz	Beth	2017-03-03	20	17	Multiple Choice	Kaplan	NULL
China Test	Karen	2017-02-04	50	45	Essay	Harris	Taylor
China Test	Alex	2017-03-04	50	38	Essay	Harris	Taylor
Grammar Test	Karen	2017-03-05	100	88	Multiple Choice, Essay	Smith	Collins

Let's first briefly describe the information that each column in this table is meant to provide. The columns are:

- **Test:** A description of the test or quiz given
- **Student:** The student who took the test
- **Date:** The date on which the test was taken
- **TotalPoints:** The total number of possible points for the test
- **Grade:** The number of points that the student received
- **TestFormat:** The format of the test: essay, multiple choice, or both
- **Teacher:** The teacher who gave the test
- **Assistant:** The person who is assigned to assist the teacher

We'll assume that the primary key for this table is a composite primary key consisting of the Test and Student columns. Each row in the table is meant to express a grade for a specific test and student.

There are two obvious problems with this table. First, certain data is unnecessarily duplicated. For example, we can see that the Pronoun Quiz, given on 2017-03-02, had a total of 10 points. The problem is that this information must be repeated in every row for that quiz. It would be better if we could simply view the total points for that particular quiz just once.

A second problem is that data is repeated within certain single cells. In the sixth row, the TestFormat is both Multiple Choice and Essay. This scenario exists because this test had both types of questions. This makes the data difficult to use. If we wanted to retrieve all tests with essay questions, how could we do that?

More generally, the main problem with this table is that it attempts to put all known information into a single table. It would be much better to break down the information in this table into separate entities, such as students, grades, and teachers, and represent each entity as a separate table. The power of SQL can then be used to join tables together as needed to retrieve any desired information.

With this discussion in mind, let's now formalize what the process of normalization hopes to accomplish. There are two main goals:

- **Eliminate redundant data.** The previous example clearly illustrates the issue of redundant data. But why is this important? What exactly is the problem with listing the same data on multiple rows? Well, besides the unnecessary duplication of effort, redundancy reduces flexibility. When data is repeated, any changes to particular values affect multiple rows rather than just one.

- **Eliminate insert, delete, and update anomalies.** The problem of redundant data also relates to this second goal, which is to eliminate insert, delete, and update anomalies. Suppose, for example, that a teacher gets married and changes her name. Because we would like the data to reflect the new name, we must now update all rows that contain her name. However, because the data is stored redundantly, we must update a large amount of data, rather than just one row.

  There are also insert and delete anomalies. For example, let's say we just hired a new teacher to teach music. We would like to record this information somewhere in the database. However, because the teacher hasn't yet given any tests, there is nowhere to put this information, because we don't have a table specific to the entity of teachers.

  Similarly, a delete anomaly would occur if we wanted to delete a row, but by doing so would eliminate some related piece of information. To use another example, if we had a database of books and wanted to delete a row for a book by George Orwell, and if that were the only book for Mr. Orwell in the database, then that row deletion would eliminate not only the book, but also the fact that George Orwell is an author of other books that might be acquired in the future.

How to Normalize Data

What, specifically, does *normalization* mean?

The term itself originates with E.F. Codd and refers to a series of recommended steps for removing redundancy and updating anomalies from a database design. The steps involved in the normalization process are commonly referred to as *first normal form, second normal form, third normal form,* and so on. Although some individuals have described steps up to a sixth normal form, the usual practice is to go through only the first, second, and third normal form. When data is in third normal form, it is generally understood to be sufficiently normalized.

We won't describe the entire set of rules and procedures for converting data into first, second, and third normal form. Other texts elaborate on the process in great detail, showing how to transform data into first normal form, then into second normal form, and finally into third normal form.

Instead, we'll summarize the rules for getting data into third normal form. In practice, an experienced database administrator can jump from unstructured data to third normal form without having to follow every intermediate procedure. We'll do the same here.

The three main rules for normalizing data are as follows:

- **Eliminate repeating data.** This rule means that no multivalued attributes are allowed. In the previous example, we cannot allow a value such as "Multiple Choice, Essay" to exist in a single data cell. The existence of multiple values in a single cell creates obvious difficulties in retrieving data by any given specified value.

  A corollary to this rule is that repeated columns are not allowed. In our example, the database might have been designed so that, rather than a single column named TestFormat, we had two separate columns named TestFormat1 and TestFormat2. With this alternative approach, we might have placed the value "Multiple Choice" in the TestFormat1 column and "Essay" in the TestFormat2 column. This would not be permitted. We don't want repeated data, whether it is represented as multiple values in a single column or as multiple columns.

- **Eliminate partial dependencies.** This rule refers primarily to situations in which the primary key for a table is a composite key, meaning a key composed of multiple columns. The rule states that no column in a table can be related to only part of the primary key.

  Let's illustrate this with an example. As mentioned, the primary key in the Grades table is a composite key consisting of the Student and Test columns. The problem occurs with columns such as TotalPoints. The TotalPoints column is really an attribute of the test and has nothing to do with students. This rule mandates that all non-key columns in a table refer to the entire key and not just a part of the key. Essentially, partial dependencies indicate that the data in the table relates to more than one entity.

- **Eliminate transitive dependencies.** This rule refers to situations in which a column in the table refers not to the primary key, but to another non-key column in the same table. In our example, the Assistant column is really an attribute of the Teacher column. The fact that the assistant relates to the teacher and not to anything in the primary key (the test or the student) indicates that the information doesn't belong in this table.

We've now seen the problems and discussed rules for fixing the data, but how are proper database design changes actually determined? This is where experience comes in. And there is generally not a single solution to any given problem.

That said, the following is one solution to this design problem. In this new design, several tables have been created from the one original table, and all data is now in normalized form. Figure 19.1 uses an entity-relationship diagram to show the tables in the new design.

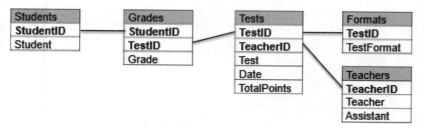

Figure 19.1   Normalized design

As mentioned in Chapter 11, entity-relationship diagrams do not display detailed data. Instead, they indicate the overall structure of the data. The primary keys in each table are shown in bold. A number of ID columns with auto-increment values have been added to the tables, allowing relationships between the tables to be defined. All other columns are the same as seen previously.

The main point to notice is that every entity discussed in this example has been broken out into separate tables. The Students table includes information about each student. The only attribute in this table is the student name.

The Grades table includes information about each grade. It has a composite primary key of StudentID and TestID, because each grade is tied to a student and to a specific test.

The Tests table has information about each test, such as date, TeacherID, test description, and the total points for the test.

The Formats table includes information about the test formats. Multiple rows are added to this table for each test to indicate whether the test is multiple choice, essay, or both.

The Teachers table includes information about each teacher, including the teacher's assistant, if one exists.

Following is the data contained in these new tables, corresponding to the data in the original Grades table.

Students table:

StudentID	Student
1	Amy
2	Jon
3	Beth
4	Karen
5	Alex

Teachers table:

TeacherID	Teacher	Assistant
1	Smith	Collins
2	Jones	Brown
3	Kaplan	NULL
4	Harris	Taylor

Tests table:

TestID	TeacherID	Test	Date	TotalPoints
1	1	Pronoun Quiz	2017-03-02	10
2	2	Pronoun Quiz	2017-03-02	10
3	3	Solids Quiz	2017-03-03	20
4	4	China Test	2017-03-04	50
5	1	Grammar Test	2017-03-05	100

Formats table:

TestID	TestFormat
1	Multiple Choice
2	Multiple Choice
3	Multiple Choice
4	Essay
5	Multiple Choice
5	Essay

Grades table:

StudentID	TestID	Grade
1	1	8
2	2	6
3	3	17
4	4	45
5	4	38
5	5	88

Your first impression might be that we have unnecessarily complicated the situation, rather than improving upon it. For example, the Grades table is now a mass of numbers, the meaning of which is not completely obvious upon quick inspection.

However, remembering SQL's ability to easily join tables together, you can also see that there is now much greater flexibility in this new design. Not only are we free to join only those tables needed for any particular analysis, but we can now also add new columns to these tables much more readily without affecting anything else.

Our information has become more modularized. Now if we decide that we want to capture additional information about each student, such as address and phone number, we can simply add new columns to the Students table. And, when we want to modify a student's address or phone number later, that change will affect only one row in the table.

The Art of Database Design

Ultimately, designing a database is much more than simply going through normalization procedures. Database design is really more of an art than a science, and it requires asking and thinking about relevant business issues.

In our grades example, we presented one possible database design as an illustration of how to normalize data. In truth, many possibilities exist for designing this database. Much depends on the realities of how the data will be accessed and modified. Numerous questions can be asked to ascertain whether a design is as flexible and meaningful as it needs to be. For example:

- **Are there other tables that need to be added to the database?** One obvious choice would be a Subjects table, which would allow for the selection of tests by subject, such as English or Math. If a Subjects table were added, it could then be asked whether we'd want to relate the subject to the test or to the teacher who administered the test.
- **Is it possible for a grade to count in more than one subject?** It might be that the English and Social Studies teachers are doing a combined lesson and want certain tests to count for both subjects. How would we account for that?
- **What do we do if a child flunks a grade and is now taking the same tests a second time?** We would need to determine how we would differentiate the student's grade for each time he took the test.
- **How do we allow for special rules that teachers might implement?** For example, a teacher might want to drop the lowest quiz score in a particular time period.
- **Does the data have special analysis requirements?** If there is more than one teacher for the same subject, do we want to be able to compare the average grades for the students of each teacher, to ensure that one teacher isn't inflating grades?

The list of possible questions is almost endless. The point is that data doesn't exist in a vacuum. There is a necessary interaction between data design and real-world requirements. Databases must be designed to allow for flexibility and ease of use. However, there is also a danger that databases can be over-designed to a point where the data becomes unintelligible. An overzealous data administrator might decide to create 20 tables to allow for every possible situation. That, too, is inadvisable. Database design is something of a balancing act in the search for a design that is sufficiently flexible but also intuitive and understandable by users of the system.

Alternatives to Normalization

We have emphasized that normalization is the overriding principle that should be followed in designing a database. In certain situations, however, viable alternatives might make more sense.

For example, in the realm of data warehouse systems and software, many practitioners advocate using a *star schema* design for databases rather than normalization. In a star schema, a certain amount of redundancy is allowed and encouraged. The emphasis is on creating a data structure that more intuitively reflects business realities, and also one that allows for quick processing of data by special analytical software.

To give a brief overview of star schema design, the main idea is to create a central fact table, which is related to any number of dimension tables. The fact table contains all the quantitative numbers that are additive in nature. In our previous example, the Grade column is such a number, because we can add up grades to obtain a meaningful total grade. The dimension tables contain information on all the entities related to the central facts, such as subject, time, teacher, student, and so on.

As an additional possibility, special analytical software can be employed that allows database developers to create cubes from their star schema databases. These cubes extend analysis capabilities, allowing users to drill down through predefined hierarchies in the various dimensions. For example, a user of such a system would be able to drill down from viewing a student's entire semester grades to seeing grades in an individual week.

Figure 19.2 shows what a database with a star schema design might look like for our grades example.

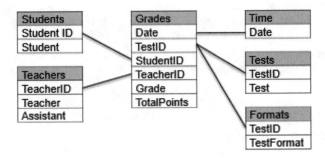

Figure 19.2   Star schema design

In this design, the Grades table is the central fact table. All other tables are dimension tables.

The first four columns in the Grades table (Date, TestID, StudentID, and TeacherID) allow each row in the fact table to be related to the corresponding row in a dimension table. For example, the StudentID column in the Grades table can be joined to a StudentID value in the Students table. The other two columns in the Grades table have additive numeric quantities. Notice that TotalPoints is now in the Grades table. In our normalized design, TotalPoints was an attribute of the Tests table and the grade was in the Grades table. By putting both the Grade and TotalPoints in a single table in this star schema design, we can more easily sum grades and compute averages (Grade divided by the TotalPoints) for any set of data.

Certainly, this is only a brief introduction to the subject of designing databases for data warehouse applications. However, it illustrates the point that there are many different ways to design a database, and the best way often relates to the type of software that will be used with the data.

Looking Ahead

This chapter covered the principles of database design. We discussed the basics of the normalization process, showing how a database with a single table can be converted into a more flexible structure with multiple tables, related by additional key columns. We also emphasized that database design is not merely a technical exercise. Attention must be paid to the organizational realities and to considerations as to how the data will be accessed and utilized. Finally, we briefly described the star schema as an alternative to conventional normalized design, in an effort to emphasize that there is often more than one feasible approach.

In our final chapter, "Strategies for Displaying Data," we'll discuss some interesting possibilities for using spreadsheets to complement our knowledge of SQL. In our quest to sharpen our SQL skills, we must not forget that there is a world out there beyond SQL. We should not expend efforts on SQL when the underlying objective can be accomplished more effectively through other means.

Strategies for Displaying Data

In this final chapter, we'll return to the main theme of this book—namely, methods of retrieving data from relational databases. In the previous few chapters, we took a detour from data retrieval to the related topics of updating data, maintaining tables, and designing databases. Now we want to focus again on the role of SQL in retrieving data. More specifically, we'll compare the capabilities of SQL to other reporting tools available to the end user and discuss strategies for employing the most appropriate tool for the job at hand.

In the broad business and corporate world, Microsoft Excel is the most widely available and pervasive reporting tool for the end user. One would be hard-pressed to find a business analyst who doesn't use or interact with Excel in some manner. In this chapter, we'll examine how Excel can be used to extend the data retrieval capabilities of SQL to further manipulate data and present it in formats that aren't easily accomplished in SQL.

Crosstab Layouts Revisited

Back in Chapter 10, we looked at using the PIVOT operator to create output in a crosstab format. In that chapter, we began with the following data in this SalesSummary table:

SalesDate	CustomerID	State	Channel	SalesAmount
4/1/2017	101	NY	Internet	50
4/1/2017	102	NY	Retail	30
4/1/2017	103	VT	Internet	120
4/2/2017	145	VT	Retail	90
4/2/2017	180	NY	Retail	300
4/2/2017	181	VT	Internet	130
4/2/2017	182	NY	Internet	520
4/2/2017	184	NY	Retail	80

Using the PIVOT operator, we created output in this crosstab format:

SalesDate	State	Internet	Retail
2017-04-01	NY	50	30
2017-04-01	VT	120	NULL
2017-04-02	NY	520	380
2017-04-02	VT	130	90

The key feature of this crosstab layout is the appearance of channel values in individual columns. Although data is grouped by SalesDate, State, and Channel, we see only combinations of SalesDate and State in the individual rows. We moved the two channel values to their own columns, Internet and Retail.

This is all fine and good, except that there was an inherent difficulty in producing output in this crosstab format. As seen in Chapter 10, the SQL statement that produced the above output was:

```
SELECT * FROM
(SELECT SalesDate, State, Channel, SalesAmount FROM SalesSummary) AS mainquery
PIVOT (SUM(SalesAmount) FOR Channel IN ([Internet], [Retail])) AS pivotquery
ORDER BY SalesDate
```

Notice that in this SQL statement we needed to specify the Channel column values, Internet and Retail, in the statement. In other words, we were required to know in advance all the possible values for the channels and put them in our statement so that columns could be created for them. As a practical matter, this is a cumbersome solution. In this simple example, with only two channel values, it doesn't seem so difficult. But in the real world, we might easily run into situations for which we might have dozens of potential values for columns, and we wouldn't know in advance what those values are.

For this reason, the PIVOT keyword is seldom used in practice. A much simpler and more powerful solution is to rely on reporting software to automatically generate reports in a crosstab format. The vast majority of reporting tools provide some sort of crosstab functionality. In Microsoft Excel, this is accomplished with pivot tables. Other reporting tools offer similar capabilities but with different names. For example, Microsoft Reporting Services provides a Matrix Report that allows the user to lay out data in a crosstab format. In SAP Crystal Reports, the crosstab report type is called a Cross-Tab.

Interestingly, the report layout in reporting tools such as Reporting Services is independent of the underlying SQL query used to retrieve data. For example, in Reporting Services, you can start with a simple SQL query without a GROUP BY clause and place that query in either a Table Report or a Matrix Report. If placed in a Table Report, the output will be a simple list of data. If placed in a Matrix Report, the data can be organized into rows and columns, and then the report will automatically perform all required grouping and generate any needed columns.

Excel and External Data

In this chapter, we'll focus on Microsoft Excel pivot tables, as this software is widely available and produces results similar to Reporting Services and other specialized reporting tools.

However, before examining the capabilities of Excel pivot tables, we need to digress for a moment into some of the possibilities for connecting to data in Excel. With its ubiquitous presence in the business world, most query and reporting tools provide a mechanism for exporting data from their tools directly into Excel. When working with SQL query tools, you generally need only to use an Export to Excel option to move data into Excel.

There are also a variety of options when working within Excel to import data from external sources. We'll focus on obtaining data from relational databases, but we will also mention in passing that Excel can also import data from text files and connect directly to OLAP databases. Text files are generally imported directly into an Excel workbook via a wizard that lets the user specify the layout of the text file, what type of delimiters are used, the properties of each column, and so on. Excel also provides the ability to connect directly to OLAP databases, sometimes referred to as cubes. When connecting to an OLAP cube, Excel uses its pivot table interface to view data in the cube.

To obtain data from relational databases, one possibility is to connect to the database server and then import data into Excel. This is generally initiated via a command under the Data tab of the Ribbon called From Other Sources. Under this command are options such as:

- From SQL Server
- From Data Connection Wizard
- From Microsoft Query

The From Data Connection Wizard allows the user to connect to databases other than SQL Server. However, we'll begin by selecting the From SQL Server option. A connection wizard appears that first asks for the database server name and logon credentials. After providing that information, we're asked to select the specific tables on that server that we would like to import. The next pane of the wizard creates an Office Data Connection (ODC) file that stores the information we specified, so that the data source can be connected to again in the future. The final step in the wizard, shown in Figure 20.1, allows us to import the data in an Excel Table, Pivot Table, or Pivot Chart.

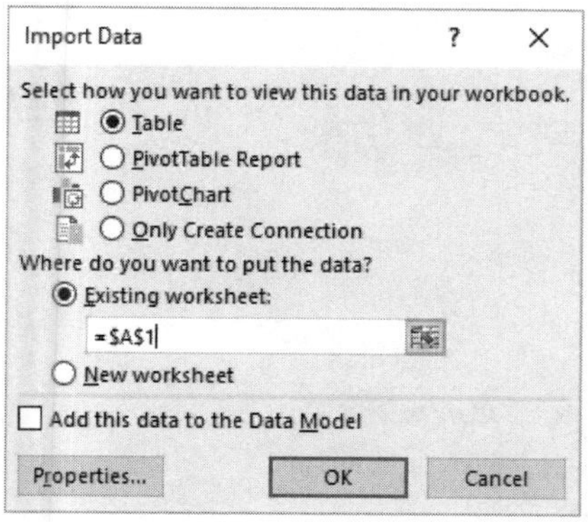

Figure 20.1   Import Data options

When selecting more than one table from the relational database, the best choice is to import the data into an Excel Table. This will import the data into Tables on multiple worksheets. If only one table was selected, then the Pivot Table or Pivot Chart is often a better choice. Of course, you can always import data into a Table and later create a Pivot Table or Chart from that Table.

The problem with this method of importing data is that it doesn't allow us to join data from multiple tables. The ability to combine data from multiple tables is easily handled in SQL, but is not so readily accomplished in Excel. This leads us to a second possibility, which is to use Microsoft Query. When selecting the From Microsoft Query option under the Data tab of the Ribbon, we are presented with a series of panes, the first of which is shown in Figure 20.2.

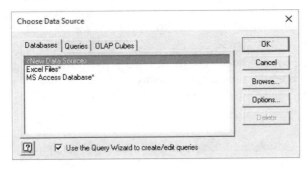

Figure 20.2   Choose Data Source

After responding to create a new data source, the next pane asks us to name the source and specify a connection driver. Behind the scenes, this connection data is saved as a Data Source Name (DSN) file, which is slightly different than an ODC file. We then click a Connect button and log in to the server. After selecting two tables from our database—for example, the Customers table and the Orders tables—the Microsoft Query window appears as in Figure 20.3.

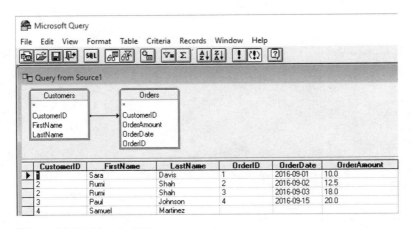

Figure 20.3   Microsoft Query

Additionally, we must manually join the two tables on the CustomerID column that appears in both tables. This is done by drawing a line to connect the columns. We also need to double-click the line to allow us to edit and specify this as an outer join between the two columns. The final step for moving this data into Excel is to select the Return Data to Microsoft Excel command under the File menu of Microsoft Query. It then shows the same Import Data options pane of Figure 20.1, allowing us to import the data into a Table, Pivot Table, or Pivot Chart. If we choose to import into a Table, the data then appears as in Figure 20.4.

CustomerID	FirstName	LastName	OrderID	OrderDate	OrderAmount
1	Sara	Davis	1	9/1/2016	10
2	Rumi	Shah	2	9/2/2016	12.5
2	Rumi	Shah	3	9/3/2016	18
3	Paul	Johnson	4	9/15/2016	20
4	Samuel	Martinez			

Figure 20.4   Excel table

We have now successfully used the Microsoft Query component of Excel to create a rudimentary query that selects data from multiple tables in a relational database and moves that data into an Excel Table. As mentioned, we can later take an additional step in Excel to create a Pivot Table from the Table. This leads us to our next topic.

Excel Pivot Tables

Excel includes many features that overlap what can be done with SQL. For example, within Excel you can sort and filter data, and apply a myriad of transformations with numerous functions. Data can also be grouped and subtotaled. But one feature of Excel that's difficult to replicate with SQL is the pivot table. Excel provides the ability to select any range of data on a worksheet and convert that data into a pivot table. Or, as discussed above, data can be imported from an external database into a pivot table.

At a basic level, a pivot table is the equivalent of the crosstab format that we've already seen. However, a key benefit of the pivot table is that it's completely interactive and dynamic. Rather than viewing a static crosstab report, you can easily modify the pivot table by rearranging data elements into its four data areas: rows, columns, values, and filters.

To better understand the tremendous capabilities of pivot tables, let's illustrate with an example. We'll start with a set of data residing in an Excel worksheet. We'll assume that the data was moved to the worksheet by utilizing a SQL statement that joined data in tables describing customers, products, and sales. The data appears in Excel as in Figure 20.5.

	A	B	C	D	E	F	G	H	I
1	Sales Date	Sales Month	Customer ID	Customer City	Customer State	Product	Product Category	Qty Sold	Total Sales
2	1/22/2017	2017-01	23	Nashville	TN	Breakfast Blend	Coffee	3	12
3	2/1/2017	2017-02	44	Seattle	WA	Vanilla	Spices	6	18
4	3/1/2017	2017-03	14	Knoxville	TN	Darjeeling	Tea	-3	-12
5	12/6/2016	2016-12	15	Atlanta	GA	Mustard	Spices	6	12
6	2/15/2017	2017-02	44	Seattle	WA	Cinnamon	Spices	8	24
7	3/6/2017	2017-03	23	Nashville	TN	Decaf	Coffee	9	36
8	2/18/2017	2017-02	18	Denver	CO	Earl Grey	Tea	4	20
9	3/31/2017	2017-03	19	Boulder	CO	Green Tea	Tea	-1	-6
10	2/6/2017	2017-02	20	Miami	FL	French Roast	Coffee	5	25
11	2/28/2017	2017-02	16	Chicago	IL	Hazelnut	Coffee	5	15
12	12/18/2016	2016-12	50	Peoria	IL	Curry	Spices	2	8
13	3/2/2017	2017-03	3	Portland	ME	Ginger	Spices	1	2
14	2/15/2017	2017-02	2	Minneapolis	MN	Oolong	Tea	8	24
15	1/11/2017	2017-01	11	Portsmouth	NH	Vanilla	Spices	4	12
16	12/27/2016	2016-12	44	Seattle	WA	Mustard	Spices	-2	-4
17	3/30/2017	2017-03	16	Chicago	IL	Vanilla	Coffee	4	16
18	1/17/2017	2017-01	49	Los Angeles	CA	Decaf	Coffee	6	24
19	2/17/2017	2017-02	22	Cleveland	OH	Green Tea	Tea	7	42
20	3/25/2017	2017-03	11	Portsmouth	NH	Oregano	Spices	10	50
21	2/18/2017	2017-02	45	Des Moines	IA	Curry	Spices	3	3

Figure 20.5   Underlying data for a pivot table

In this data, rows with negative quantities and sales represent returns. There is one row per order or return. The first step is to insert this data into a pivot table. This is accomplished by selecting the Pivot Table command under the Insert tab of the Ribbon. Accepting the default values on the Create PivotTable pane will create a pivot table as shown in Figure 20.6.

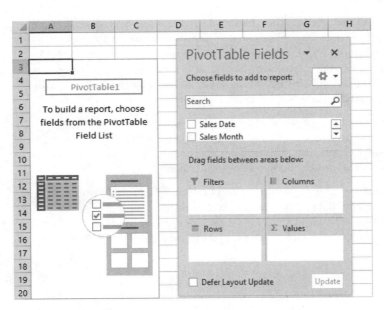

Figure 20.6   A pivot table with the PivotTable Fields list

At this point, we see an empty pivot table and a PivotTable list showing the available fields that can be moved into the pivot table. The easiest way to move data to the pivot table is to drag fields from the list to one of the four areas of the pivot table on the Fields list: Filters, Rows, Columns, or Values. Let's begin by moving Customer State to the Filters area, Sales Month to the Rows area, Product Category to the Columns area, and Total Sales to the Values area. The results are shown in Figure 20.7.

	A	B	C	D	E	F	G	H	I	J
1	Customer State	(All)								
2										
3	Sum of Total Sales	Column Labels								
4	Row Labels	Coffee		Spices	Tea	Grand Total				
5	2016-12		16			16				
6	2017-01	36	12			48				
7	2017-02	40	45	86		171				
8	2017-03	52	52	-18		86				
9	Grand Total	128	125	68		321				
10										
11										
12										
13										
14										
15										
16										
17										
18										
19										
20										

PivotTable Fields

Choose fields to add to report:

Search

☐ Sales Date
☑ Sales Month

Drag fields between areas below:

▼ Filters   Ⅲ Columns
Customer St... ▼   Product Cate... ▼

≡ Rows   Σ Values
Sales Month ▼   Sum of Total ... ▼

☐ Defer Layout Update   Update

Figure 20.7   A pivot table with fields in all four areas

Let's examine what has happened to our data. Pivot tables sum all the detailed data to which the pivot table is connected. The pivot table displays as many rows and columns as are necessary to display that data. The data is displayed in a crosstab format, with fields in the Rows or Columns areas, and quantitative values summed in the Values area. The Filter area can be used to apply a filter to everything in the pivot table. In this example, we've placed Customer State in the Filters area but haven't yet applied any filters on the state.

When fields are moved to any of the four areas, the pivot table is instantly updated with appropriate values corresponding to the new layout. It's a highly interactive device that lets you manipulate data at will.

Unlike with SQL statements, you never need to specify a grouping in pivot tables. Excel assumes that you want grouping of any fields placed in the Rows or Columns area. In this example, the pivot table has grouped all data by Sales Month and Product Category. We see, therefore, that there was a total of 86 dollars of Tea sales in the month of February 2017. Grand Total rows and columns have been added automatically, although those Grand Totals can just as easily be turned off.

If we want to group data or modify the presentation in a slightly different manner, that is easily accomplished. In this next iteration, we'll move the Sales Month to the Columns area, move the Product Category to the Rows, add Product to the Rows area, and adjust the Customer State filter to select only data from Illinois (IL) and Tennessee (TN). The resulting data is shown in Figure 20.8.

	A	B	C	D	E	F
1	Customer State	(Multiple Items) .T				
2						
3	Sum of Total Sales	Column Labels ▾				
4	Row Labels ▾	2016-12	2017-01	2017-02	2017-03	Grand Total
5	⊟Coffee		12	15	52	79
6	Breakfast Blend		12			12
7	Decaf				36	36
8	Hazelnut			15		15
9	Vanilla				16	16
10	⊟Spices	8				8
11	Curry	8				8
12	⊟Tea				-12	-12
13	Darjeeling				-12	-12
14	Grand Total	8	12	15	40	75

Figure 20.8   Rearranged pivot table with a filter applied

Notice that we now see a hierarchy of fields in the rows area. Within each product category, we see the various products that belong to that category. Sales Month values are now broken down into separate columns. Because we applied a filter by state, we now see a Grand Total of only 75 dollars in sales rather than the previous 321.

In addition to allowing summation of values, the pivot table allows other options, such as count, average, and so on. However, understand that only summable quantitative values can be placed in the Values area of the pivot table. In this sense, pivot tables are a close cousin of the star schema dimensional design discussed in Chapter 19. Whereas dimensional data can be placed in the Rows, Columns, or Filters areas, summable quantities belong in the Values area. The Values area of the pivot table is analogous to data in a Fact table of a star schema design.

In addition to allowing you to move fields at will between the areas of the pivot table, Excel also provides a few interesting Report Layout options. There are three basic layout options for pivot tables:

- Compact Form
- Outline Form
- Tabular Form

When a pivot table is selected, these options appear under the Design tab of the Ribbon. The layout in Figures 20.7 and 20.8 is Compact Form. After switching the layout of Figure 20.8 to Outline Form, the pivot table appears as in Figure 20.9.

	A	B	C	D	E	F	G
1	Customer State	(Multiple Items) .T					
2							
3	Sum of Total Sales		Sales Month ▾				
4	Product Category ▾	Product ▾	2016-12	2017-01	2017-02	2017-03	Grand Total
5	⊟Coffee			12	15	52	79
6		Breakfast Blend		12			12
7		Decaf				36	36
8		Hazelnut			15		15
9		Vanilla				16	16
10	⊟Spices		8				8
11		Curry	8				8
12	⊟Tea					-12	-12
13		Darjeeling				-12	-12
14	Grand Total		8	12	15	40	75

Figure 20.9   Pivot table in Outline Form

In the Outline Form, we now see the Product Category and Product in separate columns, with labels for each field in the header area. This format clearly lists all field names in the display.

There are many other useful features of pivot tables, but one last benefit we'll illustrate is the ability to drill down from the summarized values on the pivot table back to the original data. This is referred to as a *drillthrough*. In this example, we'll double-click the cell with the value of 40, shown as the Grand Total of sales for March 2017. When we do this, a new worksheet appears that looks like Figure 20.10.

	A	B	C	D	E	F	G	H	I
1	Sales Date ▾	Sales Month ▾	Customer ID ▾	Customer City ▾	Customer State ▾	Product ▾	Product Category ▾	Qty Sold ▾	Total Sales ▾
2	3/1/2017	2017-03	14	Knoxville	TN	Darjeeling	Tea	-3	-12
3	3/6/2017	2017-03	23	Nashville	TN	Decaf	Coffee	9	36
4	3/30/2017	2017-03	16	Chicago	IL	Vanilla	Coffee	4	16

Figure 20.10   Drillthrough results

This table of data shows the detailed data used to calculate the value of 40 in the pivot table. There are three rows shown, representing the three rows we saw previously in Figure 20.5. If we sum the values in the Total Sales column, we can verify that Total Sales in March 2015 are indeed 40.

Looking Ahead

This chapter examined a few ways in which reporting tools and pivot tables can be used to summarize data in a manner that is difficult to present strictly through SQL statements. Pivot tables in Excel use the basic concept of the crosstab report and extend it to provide additional flexibility and functionality. By being aware of reporting and analytical tools available to reformat data, SQL developers can focus their talents on retrieving data and let the reporting tool or end user handle more complex display issues.

If you haven't already done so, you may want to take a look at Appendixes A, B, and C for some tips on how to get started with Microsoft SQL Server, MySQL, or Oracle. These appendixes provide instructions on how to install the free versions of these databases and also provide some basic information on how to use the software to execute SQL commands.

At the beginning of this book, we mentioned that SQL involves both logic and language. The language component is fairly obvious. In each chapter, we stressed the keywords introduced and the meaning behind those words. But now that you've completed the book, you will hopefully better appreciate that the true power of SQL lies in the logic that it encompasses.

It is pure logic that allows you to take a bunch of values arranged in columns and rows and transform them into something approaching meaningful information. The challenge in using SQL is in determining how to apply logic to real-world data. This is where the theoretical and practical meet. By using functions, aggregation, joins, subqueries, views, and the like, the practitioner must grapple with the reality of raw data and learn how to manipulate it with a few appropriate twists of logic.

But logic isn't the end of the matter. The language of SQL plays an equally important role. In a sense, the beauty of SQL lies in the fact that its language is quite sparse. It's neither verbose nor overly cryptic. Each keyword has a distinct purpose and specifies a particular bit of logic and nothing more. We wouldn't go as far as to say that SQL has poetic qualities, but within the realm of computer languages, the language does carry a certain aesthetic appeal.

A

Getting Started with Microsoft SQL Server

The following describes the procedure for installing the free version of Microsoft SQL Server on a computer running Windows. Note that the procedure may vary, depending on what is already installed on your computer. There are two main steps:

1. Install SQL Server 2016 Express.
2. Install SQL Server 2016 Management Studio Express.

Microsoft SQL Server 2016 Express allows you to create databases. SQL Server 2016 Management Studio Express is a graphical interface that allows you to issue SQL commands to interact with the server and any databases you create.

Installing SQL Server 2016 Express

The steps for installing SQL Server 2016 Express are as follows.

1. Go to microsoft.com/en-us/server-cloud/products/sql-server-editions.
2. Under EXPRESS, select DOWNLOAD.
3. Sign in to your Microsoft account. Create an account if you don't have one.
4. Select your language, and then DOWNLOAD.
5. After the download completes, run the downloaded file. Accept the suggested download location, and then click OK.
6. Select installation type BASIC.
7. Select ACCEPT to accept the license terms.
8. Accept the install location, and click NEXT.
9. When the download completes, installation will automatically begin.
10. After installation completes, select CLOSE.

After this has completed, you will have SQL Server 2016 Installation Center installed.

Installing SQL Server 2016 Management Studio Express

The steps for installing SQL Server 2016 Management Studio Express are as follows:

1. Open the SQL SERVER 2016 INSTALLATION CENTER application that was installed with SQL Server 2016 Express.
2. Select INSTALLATION on the left pane, then INSTALL SQL SERVER MANAGEMENT TOOLS.
3. Select DOWNLOAD SQL SERVER MANAGEMENT STUDIO (SSMS).
4. After the download completes, click RUN, then INSTALL.
5. When installation completes, click CLOSE.

After this has completed, you will have several new software apps installed, including SQL Server 2016 Management Studio.

Using SQL Server 2016 Management Studio Express

When you open the SQL Server 2016 Management Studio application, you'll first see a Connect to Server window. This window allows you to establish a connection with the SQL Server 2016 Express instance that you already installed.

The Server Name will show the SQLEXPRESS instance you installed, and the Authentication will show Windows Authentication. The Server Type is Database Engine.

Click the CONNECT button.

After connecting, you'll need to create a database to work with. To do this, find the Object Explorer pane on the left side of the window, right-click the DATABASES line, and then select NEW DATABASE. In the New Database window, enter a name in the Database Name box (for example, FirstDatabase). Click the OK button. You will now see your new database under Databases.

To execute any desired SQL code, highlight your database and then click the NEW QUERY button. A new query window will open. You can enter any SQL code and then click the EXECUTE button. If you enter multiple SQL statements in the query window, you can highlight any number of individual statements and execute only the highlighted portion. The results of your query will be shown in either a Results pane or a Message pane after the query is executed. If there is data to be displayed, it will appear in a Results pane; otherwise, a status message will appear in a Message pane.

Getting Started with MySQL

The following describes the procedure for installing the free version of MySQL on a Windows or Mac computer. Note that the procedure may vary, depending on what is already installed on your computer. There are two main pieces of software to install:

1. Install MySQL Community Server.
2. Install MySQL Workbench, version 5.2 or higher.

MySQL Community Server allows you to create databases. The MySQL Workbench is a graphical interface that allows you to issue SQL commands to interact with the server and any databases you create. At the time of this writing, MySQL Community Server is at version 5.7. MySQL Workbench is at version 6.3.

Installing MySQL on Windows

This procedure will install MySQL Community Server and MySQL Workbench on a Windows computer.

The steps for installing are as follows:

1. Go to dev.mysql.com/downloads.
2. Under the MySQL Community Server heading, click DOWNLOAD.
3. Select the MICROSOFT WINDOWS platform, click the DOWNLOAD button next to WINDOWS MYSQL INSTALLER MSI, and then click DOWNLOAD again.
4. If desired, log in to an Oracle web account, or create a new account. Otherwise, click JUST START MY DOWNLOAD. After the download completes, select the RUN button. The install setup wizard will start.
5. On the License Agreement pane, accept the terms and click NEXT.
6. On the Choosing a Setup Type pane, select the DEVELOPER DEFAULT option, and then click NEXT. This will install both MySQL Server and MySQL Workbench. Click NEXT.

7. If the Check Requirements pane appears, it may note additional installs necessary to meet requirements. Click EXECUTE to install the missing software. When installation of any missing software is complete, click NEXT.

8. On the Installation pane, click EXECUTE. When installation of all software completes, click NEXT.

9. On the Product Configuration pane, click NEXT.

10. On the Type and Networking pane, accept all defaults and click NEXT.

11. On the Accounts and Roles pane, enter a password, and then click NEXT.

12. On the Windows Service pane, accept all defaults and click NEXT.

13. On the Plugins and Extensions pane, accept all defaults and click NEXT.

14. On the Apply Server Configuration pane, click EXECUTE, and then click FINISH when done.

15. On the Product Configuration pane, click NEXT.

16. On the Connect to Server pane, click CHECK to verify the root user password, and then click NEXT.

17. On the Apply Server Configuration pane, click EXECUTE. When configuration completes, click FINISH.

18. On the Product Configuration pane, click NEXT.

19. On the Installation Complete pane, click FINISH.

After the above has completed, you will have MySQL Community Server and MySQL Workbench installed.

Installing MySQL on a Mac

This procedure will install MySQL Community Server and MySQL Workbench on a Mac computer.

1. Go to dev.mysql.com/downloads.

2. Under the MySQL Community Server heading, click DOWNLOAD.

3. Select the MAC OS X platform, and then click the DOWNLOAD button next to the DMG ARCHIVE file.

4. If desired, log in to an Oracle web account, or create a new account. Otherwise, click JUST START MY DOWNLOAD. After the download completes, open the downloaded DMG file, and then open the PKG file it creates. The install setup wizard for MySQL Community Server will start. On the Introduction pane, click CONTINUE.

5. On the License pane, click CONTINUE, and then AGREE.

6. On the Installation Type pane, click INSTALL. Make note of any temporary passwords you are given.

7. On the Summary pane, you'll see a message that installation is complete. MySQL Community Server has now been installed. Click Close. If desired, this service can be stopped or restarted at any time by selecting the MySQL icon in the Mac System Preferences app.

8. Return to dev.mysql.com/downloads.

9. Under the MySQL Workbench heading, click DOWNLOAD.

10. Select the MAC OS X platform, and then click the DOWNLOAD button next to the DMG ARCHIVE file. Click again to start the download. After the download completes, open the downloaded DMG file. In the window that pops up, drag the MySQLWorkbench.app icon to the Applications folder. Wait for the copy to complete.

11. Open the Mac Systems Preferences app and click the MySQL icon. Click the button to start MySQL Server if it is not already running.

Using MySQL Workbench

When you first open MySQL Workbench after the initial install, you will need to establish a connection to the MySQL Server instance that you already installed.

To create a connection, select Connect to Database under the Database menu. On the Stored Connection dropdown, select the instance you installed, and then enter the password you created previously for your user.

After creating the connection, you'll need to create a database to work with. To do this, click the icon under the menu bar that says CREATE A NEW SCHEMA IN THE CONNECTED SERVER. Enter a desired database name, and then click APPLY. This will generate a script to create a new schema. Click APPLY to run the script. You will then see your new database under the list of schemas in the Navigator pane. You should then return to Manage Connections under the Database menu and enter the database you just created as the default schema. You can then highlight that database and create a new query to run any desired SQL against that database.

After entering a SQL statement in the Query pane, click the EXECUTE button, which looks like a lightning bolt. If you enter multiple statements in the window, you can highlight one individual statement and execute only the highlighted portion.

The results of your query will be shown under an Output or Result pane after the query is executed. If there is data to be shown, it will appear in a Result pane; otherwise, a status message will appear under an Output pane.

C

Getting Started with Oracle

The following describes the procedure for installing the free version of Oracle on a computer running Windows. In addition to Windows, this database is also available for Linux but not for the Mac. Note that the procedure may vary, depending on what is already installed on your computer. There is just one step for the install:

- Install Oracle Database Express Edition.

This installation will create a single database and provide a web-based graphical interface that will allow you to execute SQL commands against the database.

Installing Oracle Database Express Edition

This procedure will install the Oracle Database Express Edition. The steps for installing are as follows:

1. Go to oracle.com/database.
2. Under the DOWNLOADS tab, select Oracle Database 11g Express Edition.
3. Accept the license agreement, and then select the appropriate download for your computer (e.g., Windows x64, Windows x32, or Linux x64).
4. Create an Oracle account or sign in with an existing account.
5. When the download completes, click OPEN to view the files.
6. Double-click the SETUP application to start the installation.
7. On the Welcome pane of the install wizard, click NEXT.
8. On the License Agreement pane, accept the terms, and then click NEXT.
9. On the Choose Destination Location pane, accept the default location and click NEXT.
10. On the Specify Database Passwords pane, enter a password, and then click NEXT.
11. On the Summary pane, click INSTALL.
12. When the install completes, click FINISH.

After these steps have been completed, you will have software installed under the Oracle Database 11g Express Edition directory in the Start menu for Windows, where the various features are accessible via the Web-based interface. The primary application you'll use in this directory is Get Started.

Using Oracle Database Express Edition

To gain access to the Oracle database, run the GET STARTED program under the Oracle Database 11g Express Edition directory in the Start menu. This will open a Web-based application that will allow you to interface with the database. If you get an error message saying the URL isn't found, check the URL properties in the Get_Started file in the directory where you installed Oracle, and go to that URL.

Click the APPLICATION EXPRESS button.

To sign on, enter a username of SYSTEM, enter the password you specified during the install, and then click the LOGIN button.

On the CREATE APPLICATION EXPRESS WORKSPACE page, enter a database username and password. The Application Express Username should be SYSTEM.

Then log in to the new workspace you created.

You will see four icons representing different functionalities: Application Builder, SQL Workshop, Team Development, and Administration. To execute SQL, click the SQL Workshop icon.

You will then see five icons: Object Browser, SQL Commands, SQL Scripts, Query Builder, and Utilities.

To execute a single SQL statement, you can use the SQL Commands icon. This will allow you to execute a single command and see any results. If you enter multiple SQL statements, you can highlight one individual statement and execute only the highlighted portion. To execute a SQL statement in the SQL Commands window, click the RUN button.

If you want to execute multiple SQL statements but don't need to see the output, you can use the SQL Scripts icon. After selecting this icon, you can either create a new script or edit an existing script. To create a new script, click the CREATE button, and then name the script and enter the statements you want in that script. To execute, click the RUN button. After you enter the request, it will ask for a confirmation to run. Click the RUN button again. You can then see a summary of your script execution by clicking the icon under the VIEW RESULTS column.

Index